FOLLOW THE TEACHER

Making a Difference
for School Improvement

ROBERT T. HESS

ROWMAN & LITTLEFIELD EDUCATION
Lanham · New York · Toronto · Plymouth, UK

Published in the United States of America
by Rowman & Littlefield Education
A Division of Rowman & Littlefield Publishers, Inc.
A wholly owned subsidiary of
The Rowman & Littlefield Publishing Group, Inc.
4501 Forbes Boulevard, Suite 200, Lanham, Maryland 20706
www.rowmaneducation.com

Estover Road
Plymouth PL6 7PY
United Kingdom

British Library Cataloging in Publication Information Available

Library of Congress Cataloging-in-Publication Data

Hess, Robert T., 1962–
  Follow the teacher : making a difference for school improvement /
Robert Hess.
    p. cm.
  Includes bibliographical references and index.
  ISBN-13: 978-1-57886-675-5 (cloth : alk. paper)
  ISBN-10: 1-57886-675-8 (cloth : alk. paper)
  ISBN-13: 978-1-57886-676-2 (pbk. : alk. paper)
  ISBN-10: 1-57886-676-6 (pbk. : alk. paper)
  1. Teachers—Professional relationships. 2. Educational leadership.
3. School improvement programs. I. Title.
  LB1775.H454 2008
  371.1—dc22   2007022199

∞™ The paper used in this publication meets the minimum requirements of
American National Standard for Information Sciences—Permanence of Paper
for Printed Library Materials, ANSI/NISO Z39.48-1992.
Manufactured in the United States of America.

For my mother, Beatrice Hess, and my mother-in-law, Irietys Burrows—the best of teachers and friends. Their example, support, and love have shaped who I am today.

CONTENTS

HELPFUL RESOURCES
TO ENCOURAGE
TEACHER LEADERSHIP

*F**ollow the Teacher* is designed as a book that will help you implement and sustain change in your school. In addition to a final section in each chapter that includes reflection questions and real-life teacher leadership scenarios, there are staff activities throughout the book that will help teachers embark on the journey of teacher leadership. The following index shows where you can find each of the staff activities. The book concludes with responses to the teacher leadership scenarios (appendix A), and appendix B is loaded with Internet resources about teacher leadership that can be investigated on the Web.

STAFF ACTIVITIES

ACKNOWLEDGMENTS

This book would not have been possible without the ongoing interactions I have experienced with outstanding teachers throughout my career. Teaching online classes through Oregon State University has given me the privilege of connecting with teacher leaders from all over the country and across the world. Many of their stories and quotes are contained throughout this book.

In addition to the online community of contributors, I also interviewed dozens of outstanding teacher leaders. I am indebted to their willingness to share their expertise and wish I could have included stories from all of the teacher leaders I have known and worked with in recent years. The following educators have stories featured in this book: Shauna Adams, Karen Babcock, Diane Bova, Tonya Cairo, Mike Fisher, Melea Kellogg, Nancy Golden, John Hamer, Kim Hanson, Terry Hoagland, Jennifer Kelly, Dale Koger, Terri Krebs, Emily Latimer, Courtney Leonard, Damen Lopez, Shannon McCaw, Janet McFetridge, Ed Mendelssohn, Linda Mullins, Ryan Noss, Ron Otterstedt, Kirk Phillips, Erika Pinkerton, Chris Reiersgaard, Kris Richardson, Elisa Stephens, Dawn Strong, Rita Weber, Paul Weill, and Stacey Whaley. I would also like to thank Deb Jolda for some careful editing, and Tom Koerner, vice president and editorial director at Rowman & Littlefield Education, who offered many helpful suggestions during subsequent revisions of the work.

Finally, a special thank you goes to my mother, Beatrice Hess, and my mother-in-law, Irietys Burrows. I have dedicated this book to these special women. I come from a family of teachers, and you will find their stories of service and leadership included in these pages as well.

Being a teacher-leader in public service is one of the noblest aspirations on the planet. It has been a thrilling life experience for me to know and work with so many fine individuals down through the years. It is my humble hope that the lessons and stories throughout this book will inspire your life and influence the children you touch every day. Teaching *is* leading. Let the adventure begin.

INTRODUCTION

> I would like to put forth the revolutionary idea that all
> teachers can lead. Let me take the notion one step fur-
> ther: If schools are going to become places where all chil-
> dren and adults are learning in worthy ways, all teachers
> must lead.
>
> —Roland Barth, author, reformer

A few years ago, I had the privilege of attending the retirement party of a teacher who had taught in the same school for 37 years. The majority of those years were spent teaching kindergarten. The school cafeteria was jam-packed with current and former students whom this special woman had touched through the years. People came out of the woodwork for the event. There were children running everywhere. It was complete bedlam. A double-digit line formed at the microphone to give tribute to this amazing woman. As someone who has worked in schools for more than 20 years, I found it to be an absolutely thrilling experience. It was like being at a carnival.

I was in the middle of this event when it struck me: Teacher leadership *is* influence. This teacher's influence was broad and deep, and the only thing she did was show up to work each day and treat every child like the most important person on the planet. She was a leader. I was in second grade when she was my teacher, and whenever I have been asked down through the years to "think of your favorite teacher," it is Linda Mullins who comes to mind. Why was she my favorite? Because she made me feel like I was *her* favorite, and judging from the size of the crowd in that cafeteria, she must have made all her children feel that way. If you are a teacher, you are a leader.

Forty years ago, the majority of educators believed a student's address was the important factor in determining student achievement. Through ample research and by the example of schools that have broken the mold and shattered stereotypes, we now understand that teacher quality and expertise have a greater impact than school demographics, but many people still don't *believe* that is the case. This book will deliver the message again that the teacher—and specifically teacher leadership—is the critical component to achieving breakthrough results in school improvement.

However, the future of education reform must reach far beyond teacher quality. System design trumps teacher quality. Educational leaders must realize that quality instruction will emerge if the system is designed effectively, and a lot more things will emerge as well: leadership, teamwork, quality of experience, safety, a positive school climate, school improvement, and many other important components.

Though this is a book about teacher leadership and the power of teacher leadership to transform school environments, it is also a book about system design. Embedded within its pages is a blueprint for designing a system where teacher leadership flourishes. Building principals are chiefly responsible for the effective *design* of a system, and this book lays the groundwork for helping principals create the conditions that will generate teacher leadership throughout their schools. It is my hope that you will not only be inspired by the examples of teacher leadership throughout this book but also understand ways that teacher leadership can be intentionally infused into your school system.

THE RECENT HISTORY OF TEACHER LEADERSHIP

A few years back, long-standing Harvard educator and reformer Roland Barth spent some time investigating the concept of teacher leadership. He worked with more than 100 of Rhode Island's finest teachers "to share thoughts, dreams, and concerns about re-forming the place of teachers in leading their schools" (Barth, 1999, p. 6). His work with these educators became the backbone for two brilliant publications, *The Teacher Leader* (1999) and *Learning by Heart* (2001).

In *The Teacher Leader*, Barth writes that in the mid-1990s a doctoral student conducted an exhaustive analysis of more than 250 major school-reform studies. The student "reported that the most prevalent recommendation to improve our nation's schools was that teachers should take on and share much more of the leadership of their schools. Then, and only then, will schools be able to transform themselves" (Barth, 1999, p. 9).

Barth's investigation into the concept of teacher leadership was at the forefront of a movement to support and encourage teacher leaders. Teacher leadership is a hot topic in educational circles today, and it should be. It is vital to school improvement and increased staff morale—especially in times of resource reduction and increased accountability. Since Barth's initial work on the subject, many other authors have written about the need and value of teacher leadership.

Understanding the foundation of teacher leadership is a theme throughout this book, because if we can unlock the secret of what it means to be a leader, we can recognize and encourage leadership everywhere it already exists. We know that confidence is built one success at a time around what we recognize and that what we recognize gets multiplied.

The reality is that even though the power brokers of education acknowledge the need and importance for teacher leadership, for some reason, perhaps many reasons, teacher leadership is just not practiced that much in schools—at least, not in many schools. The Carnegie Foundation has listed the following areas where teacher involvement is essential to the health of a school (Barth, 1999, p. 11). How much are teachers involved in these important decisions at your school?

- Choosing textbooks and instructional materials
- Sharing the curriculum
- Setting standards for student behavior
- Placement of students into classes and instructional groupings
- Designing staff development and in-service programs
- Setting promotion and retention policies
- Deciding school budgets
- Evaluating teacher performance
- Selecting new teachers
- Selecting new administrators

In most schools and districts, teachers might have input or influence over some of these areas, but they will rarely have the ultimate decision. With leadership comes accountability and empowerment. Empowerment leads to confidence, and confidence will ultimately lead to increased educational outcomes and results.

WHAT IS TEACHER LEADERSHIP?

In writing this book over the course of four years, I posed the question, "What is teacher leadership?" to dozens and dozens of teachers, administrators, and other school personnel. They were educators at all levels, public and private, experienced and inexperienced. As you can imagine, I came across a wide variety of responses. I discovered there are two schools of thought when it comes to teacher leadership.

The vast majority of the literature on the subject portrays teacher leadership for the select few: the "superstars" of the profession who are instructional coaches or professional developers—the ones who win awards, write grants, and make the rest of the staff feel guilty for not measuring up. These are the few who achieve remarkable results in the midst of daunting circumstances and *get recognized* for it. Some of them are so special movies are made about their lives. They appear on TV, write books, and travel the speaking circuit.

The alternative view about teacher leadership suggests the radical notion that all teachers can lead (Barth, 2001), and that not only can all teachers lead but that all teachers *should* lead if schools are to reach their potential for all students. From this perspective, leadership is not just for the three teachers in the building who are on every committee and in the center of every innovation and talk the most at staff meetings. In the world according to Barth, every teacher can have a meaningful impact in schools through leadership roles.

You've probably already guessed what side of the track I come from. I believe emphatically that all teachers have the power and potential to lead, and that teacher leadership is a matter of opportunity, training, and desire. We will not have quality schools without high levels of teacher leadership.

This book is written from the perspective that all teachers can *and should* lead in some way, and that anyone can develop leadership skills that will benefit children, their colleagues, and the community at large. Since teacher leadership is a matter of opportunity, training, and desire, it is my hope that this book will inspire teachers to take on more leadership roles and help principals find ways to support teachers in leadership roles and look for opportunities to launch teachers into leadership.

My favorite definition of teacher leadership was shared with me by a high school special education teacher.

> Teacher leadership can take many forms. Teacher leaders show themselves in many ways both in and out of school. Not all teacher leaders are visible. Some do their work quietly and without fanfare. They focus on their students. They respect their peers. They recognize that diversity within the teaching profession is good. They are willing to accept change and work with it. They are constantly looking for ways to improve themselves, their classrooms, and their schools. They are patient and try to maintain their perspective, taking into account the "big picture." They accept the use of technology as an essential tool for instruction and productivity. They are not threatened by people who are more outgoing and extroverted than themselves. They actively try to get parents involved in school life. Teacher leaders inspire the people around them.

I think this teacher is on to something. Teacher leaders do inspire the people around them. Throughout this book's pages you will find the words of teachers and examples of teachers leading in a variety of ways—some small and others large. Administrators who wander through these pages will glean ideas for training and opportunities to expand teacher leadership in their buildings. When all is said and done, whether you are a teacher or an administrator, it is my hope that children in schools will benefit most of all from the words in this book.

Though educators define teacher leadership in different ways, the first step in developing teacher leadership is through conversation. It is important to find out what teachers think about leadership and come to some common ground about what it means to be a teacher leader. Teacher leadership is not reserved for future administrators or staff members who talk too much. As the above definition implies, teacher leadership can take many forms, and this book will highlight those forms. Being a teacher leader begins with wanting to make a difference in the lives of your students.

TEACHER LEADERSHIP TODAY

There are several books about teacher leadership on the market today. Why should you read this one? For two reasons: The first is that most of those books target people who have already identified themselves as leaders and who walk in leadership roles such as instructional coaches, mentors, professional developers, department heads, or coordinators. This is a book for *all* teachers. It's a book for teachers who aren't necessarily striving to be leaders but lead in subtle ways nonetheless. It contains stories of ordinary teachers who end up doing extraordinary work in ordinary ways. This is also a book for principals who are serious about school improvement and realize that the only way for real reform to hit American schools is for teachers—all teachers—to become leaders.

In times of depleting resources and increased expectations for schools, our principals and school leaders must invest in the most underutilized resource available—the development of teacher leaders. Through the development of teacher leadership, principals can multiply their influence and efforts to meet student needs. Encouraging and supporting teacher leadership can have a bigger impact than increased funding, and it can be done effectively without increased resources.

This book encourages principals to look for and tap the vast resource of teacher leadership that exists all around them. It will also motivate teachers to step in and take on leadership roles that they didn't know were available. This is a book by an educator with 20 years of experience as a teacher and a principal. It is for principals and teachers who want to make a difference in their schools, districts, and communities. It will benefit anyone who is serious about school improvement.

THE TIME IS NOW FOR TEACHER LEADERSHIP

The needs of our children are too great, and time is too critical, to leave leadership to someone else or wait for people to step forward. The increased levels of accountability and testing have added additional strain and stress to students and teachers in public schools across the country. Now, with the stakes so high, it is imperative that teachers share in the leading of their schools, for it is only through shared leadership that we have the chance to see breakthrough results for all our students. Author Elaine McEwan (2002) states,

> Leadership is influencing others to change, learn, grow, expand, move forward, do things differently, become independent, take responsibility, and achieve goals. Highly effective teachers wield this influence in three very different, but highly connected arenas: the classroom, the school, and the community. (p. 37)

Teachers need to understand that they already are leaders. They cannot even begin to manage the daily activities of the children in their charge without being leaders. The primary focus of this book, however, is not only the leadership that goes on in the classroom but also how principals can support teachers to pursue leadership roles beyond the classroom—influencing the classroom next door, the benchmark team, the rest of the rooms along the hallway, or the functioning of the entire school, the community, and beyond.

Every teacher can step into leadership roles beyond the classroom. It is important that every teacher does step into such roles, because there is too much work to be done for just a few teachers. If everyone gets involved to some degree, the load is spread throughout the school. More work will get done, and the students will benefit most of all.

It is probably not good to begin a book with an apology, so please consider this a confession. I am a dyed-in-the-wool, trench-jumping, front-line worker who prefers an hour in a classroom to a day outside it. However, my labor takes me in and out of the camps of both practitioners and consultants, and though I try to get along with everyone, sometimes I get grief from both sides. So let me be clear from the start: This book is for practitioners. Developed from the conversations and stories of dozens of teacher leaders and administrators, *Follow the Teacher* is for principals and teachers who work in schools every day. It is for people who can relate to the summer-break countdown calendar, the Friday afternoon last-bell thrill, and the Sunday night jitters when it is time to gear up for the coming week.

My first book, *Excellence, Equity, and Efficiency*, is thicker in theory and research and presents a model for quality school improvement. My second book, *Priority Leadership*, written with Superintendent Jim Robinson, will appeal to anyone—in and out of schools—interested in improving his or her leadership ability. But this book is for those who are, or want to be, teachers and principals. Learning from the stories, participating in the activities, and applying the lessons will lead to school improvement.

A teacher leader once told me about a life philosophy she learned from her grandmother, "Touch what you can reach." In the garden of life, we each are given a little corner. This book will give you tools to make your patch of ground a little better, and as you step into leadership roles in your school, you will find your influence touching the lives of others and making the world a better place. Enjoy.

1

EVERY TEACHER IS A LEADER

> I believe that a school cannot become great if it only has a
> few good leaders. . . . Everyone involved with the school
> needs to be a leader. They need to find what they are pas-
> sionate about and pursue how to make it work. If every-
> one in the school takes a leadership role, a school can re-
> ally become what we want it to!
>
> —Middle School Science Teacher

A new teacher walked into her first classroom for the first time. She wondered all day long when the "real teacher" would come and get the class. It took a few days for the immensity of it all to sink in. Then it dawned on her that *she* was the real teacher, and that someone had thought enough of her to declare her to be the *real teacher.* She came to the realization that it's not until you take the helm that you are, in fact, sailing the boat. The teacher is the captain of her classroom, and it is precisely her effectiveness as a leader that will determine whether that class sails, sinks, or drifts somewhere in between. Teacher leadership begins in the classroom.

Since teachers are captains, their crew is the children in their charge day after day. In the classroom journey toward undiscovered lands of learning, it is the teacher who is chiefly responsible for a safe and successful passage. To be a teacher is to be a leader. No one can be effective as a teacher for very long if he or she doesn't know how to lead. Leading is the foundation of teaching, and learning is the foundation of leading. Teachers must know where they are going (standards) and how to get there (lesson plans and curriculum). They must also know how to decide whether or not their students are getting there (assessment), and what to do if their students are not making it or are ready to move ahead of the group (differentiation). Yes, teachers are leaders—for better or for worse—and good teachers are, invariably, good leaders.

Though the teacher leadership movement is gaining momentum across America, many teachers tend to shy away from this concept of leadership. When the idea of teacher leadership is mentioned to teachers, most of them immediately think of someone else. The majority of people become teachers not because they want to lead but because they want to serve—they want to help children. And therein lies the paradox: the most effective leaders *are* servants.

SERVANT LEADERSHIP

In the leadership literature, the concept of servant leadership was first proposed by Greenleaf (1977), and later developed by several others including Hunter (1998), Autry (2001), and Blanchard (2003). The concept of servant leadership is relatively simple: the most effective leaders are known primarily for their service (Greenleaf, 1977). These leaders are not self-seeking, power-grabbing ladder climbers. They are the ones willing to get down and do the dirty work that others are not willing to do.

They do not take on leadership roles to be recognized, and many times their best work never gets noticed. They are not interested in the limelight. They are the Mother Teresas of the next generation. Mother Teresa didn't work out of desire for recognition. When she became famous, she didn't leave the slums of India for the speaking circuit. She kept working—side by side with the people she had come to help when she started 50 years earlier. Servant leaders rarely become famous, and that's fine with them. They take their pleasure in serving, and paradoxically, they point the way more clearly than anyone else. They become beacons of light attracting and benefiting all those who are near them.

The most effective teachers are servant leaders. They work tirelessly, day after day—alone for the most part—in the obscurity of their classrooms. Administrators may pop in from time to time, and parents may visit to help and support, but it is the teachers who are serving. It is the teachers who are leading.

SERVICE IN ACTION

In my days as a principal, I once worked with an extremely effective primary reading teacher. He was one of the most remarkable servant leaders I ever had the privilege of working with. He was an unassuming man with a wealth of information and knowledge about reading strategies and interventions to help young readers, and he was committed and dedicated to the growth and learning of each child in his charge. He didn't like the limelight. He was not an expert at public presentations, but I learned to depend on him whenever I needed some honest feedback. However, he rarely gave that feedback unless he was asked. I never regretted going to his well of knowledge for nourishment and support, and I will never forget the year he saved our school's state testing program.

The state department of education was piloting a new method of online state assessment that could only be accessed through computers. The theory was great. Online testing enabled students more than one opportunity to take the test. The test could be administered when the student was ready. Students could take the assessment over several days and at their own pace. At my school we liked the idea so much we signed up for the online assessment even though we didn't have the computers to support it adequately. We struggled throughout the entire school year with old, hand-me-down machines that we scrounged together from auctions and the local neighborhood. Technical support was weak to nonexistent from the district office at the time, and we did just about everything ourselves.

Even though it was not part of his job description, this reading specialist stepped up to help keep our oddball collection of machines running so that state testing could happen, but it was becoming clear as the year rolled on that we would not be able to test all of our students without a serious influx of machines. Quietly and without fanfare, our servant leader stepped up to save that first year's testing. During spring vacation, he cleaned out his funds to purchase 11 new machines from a local vendor. To the consternation of the downtown tech warlords, he set up those machines on his own over spring break.

Sometimes servant leaders sidestep policy when the need is great. Without those machines, the testing never would have occurred properly.

We were able to finish testing that spring by rotating all of the students through the new mini-lab that was shoehorned together, and the results the students obtained were a highlight of the school year. That reading specialist didn't have to do what he did, but his commitment to the school and children to meet the need at hand was inspiring.

His service eventually even inspired the tech services department to a higher level of support and service for the school, which is precisely what acts of service and leadership do—they inspire similar responses in others. Servant leaders rarely complain, always seem willing to help, and stay positive even in the most trying of situations. Helping teachers recognize they are exhibiting the highest form of leadership when serving others is an important way to build confidence, and confidence is the key to building leadership capacity in teachers.

THE POWER OF CONFIDENCE

Helping teachers realize the ways they *are leaders* right now, today—and how important that leadership is—will build their confidence to take on more leadership roles in the future. Confidence has a positive snowballing effect in organizations. In organizations with high levels of confidence, people feel good about coming to work each day. There is a positive, can-do attitude in the building. Teachers are willing to step out, try new things, and take risks they normally wouldn't take.

Harvard business professor Rosabeth Moss-Kanter documents the power and importance of confidence in her book *Confidence: How Winning Streaks and Losing Streaks Begin and End* (2004). After studying successful businesses, sports teams, and educational institutions for several years, she came to the conclusion that the single most important difference between successful organizations and unsuccessful organizations was *confidence*. The winners had it. The losers didn't.

> The pattern is consistent everywhere, from the sports world to the business world to education, and to every realm in which individuals perform to high standards. In the midst of winning cycles, people naturally gravitate toward behaving in ways that support confidence. (p. 46)

Encouraging teachers to take initiative and supporting them when they do are key elements in building confidence and developing teacher leaders. Principals who encourage and expect risk taking by their staff will find them more and more willing to step out and make a difference.

Each year I teach online classes on teacher leadership through the Mentored Masters program at Oregon State University. Students from all over the country are enrolled in the course, and through this 10-week experience, all of the teachers grow in their confidence to take on leadership roles. Notice how big a role confidence played in helping shift this student's thinking about teacher leadership by the end of term:

> I am ready to take on the world, or at least the school, as a leader. I am excited to take some risks and maybe a little less apprehensive to try new things. I thought being a teacher leader was something just a few people did. They took on an extra job here or there but I know now that we all can be part of it. Even vowing to read all articles on school policy, change, money issues, etc. is taking a leadership role. Being in the know is most important of all.

LEADERS ARE LEARNERS

As the student achievement leader for Springfield Public Schools, I have the privilege of working with some of the finest teachers in the state of Oregon. Springfield is a blue-collar city located in the South Willamette Valley. The city of Eugene and the University of Oregon are our neighbors to the west, and the 11,000 students in our district attend 13 different schools throughout the city. We also have four small country schools located in rural areas outside of the city.

These four country schools have student populations between 50 and 175 students, and due to their small size, they don't have a principal on site. A principal from one of the other elementary schools is assigned to each school, but obviously, they don't have a lot of time to spend in the building. To help support the management of the schools, one of the teachers at each school is designated as the "head teacher." This teacher leader teaches full time with the support of a half-day substitute once a week to help him or her manage the school. Each of these teacher leaders demonstrates leading through learning. No matter how many years these teachers have taught, they are always pursuing new ways to teach and new things to try. They are learners.

In an effort to increase learning through the use of technology in our schools, the district piloted the use of handheld assessment devices. We initially had ten sets to deploy throughout the district, and when the head teacher at one of our country schools found out a set was available, she immediately got her hands on one of the systems. She was also piloting a new computerized math program at the same time. At first I was a little worried that she was taking on too many innovations at once. Trying to get 30 second- and third-graders in a blended classroom to meet state standards in itself is a daunting task, and this teacher was not a digital native.

Employing all of this technology at once was not easy for her, but she put her fears aside and pursued the innovations because she saw an opportunity to help her students learn and achieve. She jumped in with some training and called for help whenever she got stuck. The result was incredible. She soon became not only a high-end user in both programs but inspired other staff members at her school to follow her example. When her school community started to see the results and levels of engagement in the students, they rallied around her and raised over $25,000 to purchase 39 laptop computers for the students so the technology could be expanded. Leaders learn. Learning leads to innovation, and innovation generates results.

LEADERSHIP OPPORTUNITIES

A middle school instructional coach once told me, "If all students can learn, then all teachers can lead." She was right, but I'd like to take her statement one step further by saying if we want all students to learn, then all teachers *must* lead—in some way. Teachers are leaders.

One of the most effective things a principal can do at the start of every school year is talk about the power of teacher leadership and share the vision of spreading out the responsibilities of leadership through committee involvement. Recruitment to committee work is tricky because many teaching contracts spell out that committee participation (leadership) is voluntary, and there usually isn't any extra money for those who "volunteer." Team or committee work in schools has a variety of names in different buildings and states across the country, but the purposes are usually pretty similar.

The list of committees below was developed through my experience in schools and research on teacher leadership. This list is not exhaustive. It serves only as a starting point to help you think about ways you can support teacher leadership at your school. Encouraging teachers to get involved in committees and supporting their involvement in a variety of ways are vital to seeing teacher leadership develop in your school and district.

After-School Programs

I have seen after-school programs meeting student needs in remarkable ways with no additional funding. In one program, instructional assistants led clubs. The last 45 minutes of their day was spent in small-group instruction after school. Though teachers developed the curriculum for the program, the assistants were central in delivering the lessons and leading the students in their groups. Classified staff felt empowered and saw significant growth and progress in their needy students.

The assistants not only had ownership over the program and deep connections with the students, but they also improved their skills in leading small-group instruction during the regular day. Interested teachers also had an opportunity to start clubs of their own where they could pursue topics they cared deeply about like writing, foreign language, science, or art. Working with interested, motivated students in a subject of their choice is teacher leadership in action, and it can be extremely rewarding and beneficial for everyone involved.

Attendance Committee

Student achievement is directly linked to school attendance. State and federal accountability systems usually target attendance in some way. Having a group of teachers meet once a month to review attendance records of students and hear concerns from grade-level teams can be extremely powerful and effective. Not only can the attendance committee design intervention and supports for students with chronic attendance and tardy problems, but they can also dream up schoolwide incentive programs that will make a positive difference. In every school there are teachers concerned about doing something to improve attendance. Empower these teachers by letting them form a committee and watch student attendance improve.

Before-School Programs

Programs of this nature can get parents and students into the school to build community and support. Even in very poor communities, "Donuts for Dads" and "Muffins for Moms" activities increase parent involvement. Parents come in to the school once a month and enjoy snacks while their child reads to them. Before-school homework and reading clubs can help struggling students stay on track. When these programs are supported by teacher leaders, the results are limitless.

Grade- and Benchmark-Level Teams

Teams of teachers working with similar content are absolutely critical to increasing student achievement and establishing teacher leadership. Roland Barth (2001) was known for stating that "teachers talking to teachers" is the most effective form of professional development.

Teachers have an amazing wealth of content and skill knowledge. Providing time for them to share information about teaching and learning is critical for high levels of student achievement. Teacher leaders are central to the establishment of professional learning communities among their peers. Effective principals ensure this kind of dialogue occurs on a regular basis, and they use the concepts of teacher leadership to support it.

Site Council/Leadership Team

Most schools have some sort of leadership or site council responsible for helping the school improve. Teacher leaders play key roles on these councils because their experience in the classroom goes a long way in determining what is possible to achieve. Principals should work hard to make sure their leadership councils are high-functioning collections of leaders who systematically analyze data and develop strategies that lead to sustained improvement that can be measured and reported to all school stakeholders.

Student Assistance Teams

Student assistance teams meet on a regular basis to discuss students who are struggling academically or behaviorally and need help or support in some way. Teachers are the key players in the teams' success because they deeply know their students. Through their expertise, they are able to design and implement interventions for struggling students to ensure their success.

Other Leadership Opportunities

Many other opportunities exist for teachers to demonstrate leadership. Options include safety committees, recycling clubs, school and district curriculum committees, crisis response teams, climate and schoolwide behavior teams, multicultural clubs, fund-raising, social committees, parent/teacher clubs, read-at-home clubs, staff development teams, special events and assemblies, scheduling committee, service learning clubs, community service projects, SMART reading programs, intramural coordination, science and poetry clubs, school newspapers and yearbooks, documenting the year on film, talented and gifted committees, Title planning teams, student government, technology committees, and many, many more.

It would be impossible to list all of the opportunities. They are as vast as the range of diverse schools. The important thing is not so much what committees are functioning in your school as who is involved. In schools with high morale and strong cultures, all teachers are involved and displaying leadership in many different ways. Effective principals harness this energy and use it to increase teacher leadership throughout their building.

If you have found ways to successfully encourage teachers to step into leadership roles or have discovered opportunities that have been successful in your school or district, please visit www.breakthrough schools.org and share your success under the tab marked "Schools." The needs in public education are too great for us not to be engaged in networking, sharing successes, and asking others for help.

The hounds of NCLB are barking at our heels. The threshold guardians of accountability do not sleep. There has never been a more essential time in the history of education than now to reach out and frequent the marketplace of ideas—bringing your wares and obtaining the produce of others. Sharing your successes and struggles with others is one of the simplest and most profound ways to generate improvement. Take time to do it. You students will be the biggest beneficiaries.

REFLECT AND RESPOND

What are some of the committees and leadership opportunities that exist for teachers at your school? What would you like to exist that doesn't right now?

TEACHER LEADERSHIP SCENARIO #1:
AN UNINVOLVED STAFF

You are the principal, and the teachers at your school seem disinterested and unmotivated to lead or learn. They don't all come to staff meetings, have lots of excuses for not coming, and definitely don't want to be there when they do come. There is quite a bit of negativity every time you mention a new project or idea. There are a few teachers who are willing to step up for committee involvement and take on leadership roles, but they are by far the minority. How do you go about inspiring leadership with a disinterested staff?

Think about what you would do and then turn to appendix A: Teacher Leadership Scenario Responses for suggestions about how to respond to the scenario listed above.

2

CULTURE IS INTENTIONAL

I remember one year in particular where I actually looked
forward to Monday, and going back to school all *weekend*!
I still talk about that year, and thinking back to it—it was
the best year I've ever had, hands down. I know a significant factor was the principal I worked for at the time, and
the culture he created.

—High School Language Arts Teacher

Teachers are directly responsible for the culture created in their classroom. Culture is intentional, and effective teachers monitor and influence the culture of their classrooms so that positive interactions and
healthy relationships are constantly occurring. They not only persistently
assess the culture in their classrooms but also work to make that culture
positive and encouraging.

Successful teachers know how to lead their students to successful
outcomes and create classroom environments that support their vision.
Teacher leaders, however, are different. They step outside their classrooms and look beyond their realm of control to influence the school
and community. They do this both informally and formally by taking on
additional roles and responsibilities.

Effective principals know that having a positive culture is paramount to student achievement, improvement, and the development of
teacher leaders. These principals understand that developing teacher
leadership is their responsibility and realize that teacher leadership will
not emerge in a school to any noticeable degree without the existence
of a positive culture. There is no "chicken and egg" debate. A positive

culture comes first. Teacher leadership will grow along with positive changes in the school culture. Change begins with intention.

CREATING A POSITIVE SCHOOL CULTURE

The entire culture of a school building can get transformed within one year—for better or worse—based upon the quality of the administrator in charge. While it is true that someone with extensive school experience can get a feel for the culture of a building just by walking through it, I've always been able to tell the most about a school's culture by listening to the principal.

Principals who brag about staff like they are family members generally have wonderful school cultures. When a principal talks about staff dedication, accomplishments, expertise, and ways they go above and beyond to meet student needs, chances are a great culture exists. Principals who build positive cultures do not bad-mouth staff members. First and foremost, they support the staff, and if performance issues arise, the effective principal will work behind the scenes with staff members, treating them with dignity and respect.

During my administrative training, I spent a week at a K–8 school under the tutelage of a phenomenal leader. He was an "old-school" principal. Discipline came first. Structure and order was paramount, but the tough exterior didn't mask his heart for kids or his support for staff. I will never forget his number one operating rule for managing staff: "Support them until your belly caves in." He lived that phrase, and the culture he created through his unconditional support was one of supreme trust. Those staff members would walk through fire for their principal, and in today's pressure cooker of accountability, a principal needs a staff willing to attempt miracles for students. I was so impressed after my time at that school I went back to my classroom and made a 30-foot poster that stated, "THIS IS A LEARNING ENVIRONMENT." I put extra effort into creating a culture of learning in my classroom for the rest of the year.

The culture of a school doesn't just "happen." It is not an accident. It may be inherited, but it is not unalterable. It may be neglected but, like a garden, it can be cultivated and nurtured. School culture is always moving in a direction, and the principal is chiefly responsible for which direction it is going.

Edward Deming (1986), the father of the quality movement, stated that management is 85 percent responsible for the system or culture of the workplace that exists. Understanding that the principal is chiefly responsible for the culture of the school is the first step to improving it, and improving it is the first step to developing teacher leadership. Culture is intentional. Effective leaders intentionally influence it.

Negative cultures are like bad viruses. Nobody wants to catch them, and they can be hard to shake. Roses don't grow in concrete, and teacher leadership will not emerge to any meaningful degree in a school with a negative culture. School culture is a function of building leadership, and determining the health of a school culture is as easy as taking your temperature. The symptoms of positive and negative cultures are easy to spot. Notice what these teacher leaders say about discerning a school culture:

School culture is essential for success. I've worked in a number of schools both as a sub and regular teacher. Generally, if the people in the building feel good about where they are, good things happen. Culture is almost palpable. I can tell almost immediately when I'm in a place where people aren't happy. School culture is something that needs to be fostered and maintained. Simple things can make or break your culture. When in doubt, always say hello to the people who pass you in a hallway. Simple courtesy can go a long way. I also find that being consistent helps. People feel comfort in not being surprised, especially when you're in a leadership role. (High School Teacher)

I believe school culture can either make or break a school. A school with a positive culture has successful, eager-to-learn students. Teachers work together, mentor others, and work closely with administration. In a negative school culture you might see out-of-control students who are not very excited about learning. The teachers might complain and feel like they have no say in any decisions regarding the school, and therefore, teachers will feel no ownership of the school. Teacher leaders have a big impact on a school's culture. (Elementary School Teacher)

I know that our school culture is mostly positive because I look forward to coming to work each day. (Middle School Teacher)

ASSESSING YOUR SCHOOL CULTURE

Since identifying ways a school culture can improve is vital to the development of teacher leadership, is there a simple, research-based, yet comprehensive way to take your school's "culture temperature"? Knowing that in a negative culture teachers rarely step into leadership roles—and seldom stay in those roles if they do—how can school leaders begin to assess their school culture needs? Are there tools available that we can use to gauge school culture more accurately than how a person feels walking down the hallway, whether or not she is happy coming to work each day, or what the principal may say about staff?

Simple Web searches reveal several tools and survey instruments for assessing a school culture, but are these tools research based, and even more importantly, do they offer a prescription for improving your school culture, if necessary? The Web Resource section of this book (appendix B) lists websites where you can find a range of school culture assessment tools.

Chris Ward, Penelope Masden-Copas, and others at the Center of Improving School Culture have developed the most efficient and effective tools I have seen for evaluating and improving a school's culture. The people at www.schoolculture.net have been studying school culture for more than 20 years—before and after it was a fad—and have developed a brief, 17-question survey that enables a building staff to quickly assess the health of their school's culture. Their survey is called "School Culture Triage" and is organized around the themes of Professional Collaboration, Affiliative Collegiality, and Self-Determination/Efficacy.

The Professional Collaboration section measures the degree to which teachers work together on curriculum, behavior systems, scheduling, time, and planning. Affiliative Collegiality refers to traditions, celebrations, and whether a sense of "community" exists among staff. A staff's sense of empowerment and their willingness to work through issues, try new strategies to solve ongoing problems, and move toward resolution rather than blame are all measured by the Self-Determination/Efficacy portion of the assessment.

What makes this research-based survey so effective is the fact that a large sampling of schools have used it to not only assess the health of their culture but also to conduct "culture audits" of their building to determine where and when they can make specific improvements to their culture. The survey includes a range of scores giving site councils, leadership teams, and principals an idea of a school's position on the continuum of a healthy school culture, and what steps a team can take to improve it.

TRANSFORMING SCHOOL CULTURE: EFFECTIVE BUILDING MANAGEMENT

Since school culture is the linchpin for the emergence of teacher leadership, finding a way to assess your school culture is important. Doing something about it is even better. Improving the school culture begins with effectively managing the building. In my first high school assistant principalship, I had the privilege of working with a seasoned, masterful administrator. He was the ultimate manager: efficient, effective, and thorough. He earned the nickname "The Brief" because he ran staff meetings with such efficiency no one ever complained. He was almost too efficient—if there can be such a thing. You never went to him with a problem or concern you didn't want action on, because he would get on it, and get it done—right away.

He was practically omnipresent in his campus supervision. If you were in his office having a conversation, and the passing bell rang, he would bolt out of his chair in midsentence and get to the hallways. He believed an ounce of prevention was worth a pound of cure, and it was far less time consuming. Action items didn't sit in committees for months without resolution under his leadership. Decisions were made and followed through, and his effective management of a large high school created a culture of trust, safety, and respect that enabled teachers to feel safe to step out of their comfort zones and take on leadership roles.

SCHOOLWIDE BEHAVIOR SYSTEMS

When it comes to creating a positive school culture, it is important to determine methods to address safety and respect. There are countless classroom and school management philosophies available across the country, and each one promises to be effective. However, there are very few systems of schoolwide behavior support that not only describe student expectations but also focus on how the adults in the school can teach and support positive expectations for student behavior. Positive Behavior Support (PBS) is just that kind of system.

The comprehensive system is described in the book *Best Behavior* by Golly and Sprague (2005). Developed by researchers at the University of Oregon and explained in detail at www.pbis.org, PBS focuses on teaching the adults in the system how to be positive, consistent, and encouraging when it comes to managing student behavior. The most exciting element of PBS is that teams of school-based teachers and administrators learn together the principles of PBS, and then apply those principles to the uniqueness of their school setting. Implementing PBS is a crash course in developing teacher leaders because it requires teacher leadership to implement the system effectively.

The effective implementation of PBS has transformed the culture of thousands of schools across the country into safe, respectful, and responsible environments. Entire state departments of education have adopted PBS as a way of universally teaching behavior expectations. Having been involved in both successful and unsuccessful PBS implementations, I will tell you emphatically that neither PBS nor any other school culture retooling will launch successfully or be sustained without effective management and leadership from the principal's office. The door of teacher leadership is opened through effective building management, and when principals become instructional leaders, teachers will begin to go through that door with greater consistency.

TRANSFORMING SCHOOL CULTURE: INSTRUCTIONAL LEADERSHIP

From day one, a principal can be a successful building manager, and the results are seen and felt immediately. The master schedule gets developed on time. Student schedules get entered and printed. Newsletters go home when they are supposed to. Classroom observations occur. Paperwork gets completed. Budgets are developed and followed. E-mails get responses and phone calls get returned. The office communicates with staff. Visitors get a friendly greeting, and a human answers the phone when you call. Things get done when they are supposed to get done. In other words, the trains run on time.

In environments where teacher leadership flourishes, however, more than just good management happens from the office. There is also a great deal of instructional leadership. Unlike building management, though, instructional leadership cannot happen overnight. Brilliant ideas and the people who bring them may show up overnight, but instructional leadership is more than good ideas and flash-in-the-pan smart principals.

Instructional leadership is making those ideas happen and getting them to take root in the system. Implementation is intense work that only occurs when people are committed for the long haul. Instructional leadership is not for the faint of heart. The proof of instructional leadership is not found in ideas getting shared—that is only the starting line. Instructional leadership is determined by what gets implemented and sustained over time with results that can be measured.

A SCHOOL WITHOUT GRADES: INSTRUCTIONAL LEADERSHIP IN ACTION

In the East Willamette Valley of rural Oregon there is a K–8 country school with an enrollment of around 250 students. The school is similar to many rural schools scattered across the landscape of the United States, but a few minutes inside the building reveal how different this school truly is. In the age of state and national grade-level testing, Lacomb School sits out there like a proud thumb, fashioning itself as a school without grade levels.

Spread throughout the school are classrooms that represent a variety of spaces attached with skill-level designations. The school is divided into three benchmarks of learning, and each benchmark has different levels. Students progress through the levels during their time at the school, with each student having the option of progressing more rapidly or taking more time depending on his or her individual learning needs. Lacomb School truly understands the meaning of continuous progress where achievement is the constant and time is the variable. The school operates in the rare place where retention and social promotion have been eliminated.

In such a model, success is the guaranteed destination for all—it just may take some students a little longer to get there, and they may need more support along the way. The mastermind behind Lacomb's gradeless system of teaching and learning is their principal, who has been at the school for nearly ten years. He is an instructional leader, and his leadership in the area of instruction has inspired his teachers to step into leadership roles as well.

When this principal leaves the school, the model he developed will live on because he has created a culture where teachers feel supported to innovate and students and parents know that the staff have the children's best interests at heart. Sustainability when leaders depart is the number one sign of effective instructional leadership and growing teacher leadership. Taking risks is another. Lacomb School can be visited at www.lebanon.k12.us/schools/lac/lac.htm.

PUTTING THE ARTS ON CENTER STAGE

A drama teacher was looking for a challenge. Having heard of start-up grant money for new small high schools, he envisioned a magnet high school that would focus on integrating academics and art throughout the entire curriculum. Beyond having an idea, he really didn't know what he was getting into. The idea was written up and found funding through the Meyer Memorial Trust and the Gates Foundation.

Walking away from the kingdom he had created at his former high school to venture into the unknown was extremely risky, but he was driven and compelled by the possibility of what could be. Over time he was able to gather some like-minded individuals, and soon they developed a vision for the curriculum. It was demanding, pioneering, innovative, and risk-taking work, but after a year and a half of planning the Academy of Arts and Academics (A3) opened in the fall of 2006 with 88 students—many of whom had experienced little success in traditional schools.

Initial results from the school are compelling. With a daily 55-minute writing period, 90-minute integrated academic courses in Humanities (English and social studies) and Inquiries (math and science) every morning, and afternoons comprised of drama, art, and music with a variety of guest artists who serve as adjunct faculty, the A3 staff is finding student motivation, engagement, parent involvement, student achievement, and grades skyrocketing.

A culture of achievement has been created, and all staff at the school live by the simple motto "Everyone learns, everyone teaches, everyone leads," and that adage applies to the students as well. The A3 experience is showing us that perhaps the biggest disconnect in the typical high school model is relevance, and that once high school students experience learning connected to their personal interests, achievement soars.

The other turnkey they've discovered for achievement is the supreme value of relationships. The relationship drum gets beaten often by today's reformers, but that doesn't mean the rest of us are listening, and it certainly doesn't mean we have changed our behavior to do something about it. At A3, they are not just talking about it. Through four-year advisories that focus on writing, every student is known. By making a commitment to phone a parent's home or work every time a student is absent, they are making a statement: "School matters." By intimately getting to know students and families, A3 staff have created a culture of relationship and connection.

With the foundation of relevance and the support of relationships, the notion of requiring rigor works in a school. Reform efforts that start with rigor by demanding higher expectations will see only minimal results unless they provide the support necessary to meet the higher standards. A3 has built in support via relevance and relationships. Results will follow; they have created a culture that virtually guarantees it. The A3 team of dreamers can be visited on the web at www.athree.org.

INTERNATIONAL HIGH SCHOOL: TEACHER LEADERSHIP AT WORK

One of the most remarkable modern examples of creating a culture that fosters teacher leadership through instructional leadership lies in the story of International High School. More than 20 years ago, a group of language arts and social studies teachers were frustrated with the lack of rigor in their high school curriculum. No big news there; many teachers could say something similar about the curriculum at their school. What is remarkable is what happened next. These teachers decided to do something about it, and they did it without grant funds, before reform dollars, and with little administrative leadership. They simply asked for permission to innovate, to dream.

Envisioning the importance of cultivating "global citizens" years before the rest of the planet caught on, these teachers developed an intensely integrated and extremely rigorous curriculum that required team teaching and joint curriculum design in language arts and social studies throughout grades 9–12. Integrated units of study culminated in demonstrations and celebrations of learning. An articulated program of study emerged. Fueled by teacher leadership and driven by student choice via applications for entry, the intensely rigorous program has become a huge success. Over the next 20 years, every high school in the district made room for the program. International High School eventually had a student body of over 1,500 students located on five different campuses. Students enrolled into the articulated curriculum spend half of their school day in the required courses of the program and are able to earn a coveted International Baccalaureate diploma for their efforts.

International High School was founded by teacher leaders who were given the right mix of autonomy and support, and the entire reform effort still exists as a flat organization completely run by teacher leaders. The staff have established elaborate protocols for making decisions regarding governance, curriculum, staffing, and budget. Staff and leadership meetings are designed so that everyone's voice is heard and respected before moving forward in a given direction.

By building everyone's capacity through the multiplication of teacher leaders, International High School is a model for high school reform with a track record of success. It was established more than 20 years ago without fanfare, reform dollars, or any of the other trappings that slow down innovation—like start-up money that dries up after the grant is awarded. The staff have planted their success in the soil of teacher leadership, and as a result they have a strong culture of empowerment, possibility, and ownership. International High School is a fascinating study of what can be accomplished when the people doing the work are given freedom to innovate and the support to achieve. In-

ternational High School can be visited on the web at http://schools
.4j.lane.edu/ihs/.

TRANSFORMING THE COMMUNITY CULTURE:
WELCOME TO CAMELOT

Teachers are responsible for the culture in their classroom. Principals are
responsible for the culture in their school. Superintendents are responsible for the culture in their district. In July of 2003, Dr. Nancy Golden
became the superintendent of Springfield Public Schools. Unlike many
new superintendents, Nancy began her career in Springfield by listening.
She listened to anyone and everyone who had something to say. She
spent her first year listening to the community and created a collective
vision that became known as the S–QEM (Springfield's Quality Education Model). The S–QEM reflects the heartbeat of the community, and
Nancy was smart enough to respond to that heartbeat. But she did more
than create a vision. She also reflects upon that vision every year in the
annual report, "How Are the Children?" Nancy's responsiveness to the
needs of the community has won them over.

Staff satisfaction is at an all-time high. How many superintendents
can say they've received a standing ovation before and after their welcome back speech to staff with both certified and classified employee
groups? After witnessing her 2006 speech, one community member re-
marked, "Nancy Golden is a rock star." It sure seems that way.

Through her visibility, availability, and constant communication,
she has changed the culture of a community. Organizations and families
in Springfield now see public education as a solution to the needs of the
community—not a problem to be fixed, monitored, or controlled.

During a recent bond measure survey, the company that performed
the survey came back to district leadership and asked, "Who is Nancy
Golden and what is she doing to make such a positive impact in the
community? We conduct surveys all over the country and we have never
had the kind of positive response to a superintendent like we have heard
about Nancy Golden. The community loves her." Yes, they do.

Nancy believes in people. She supports them. She goes the extra
mile for others and, as a result, people go the extra mile for her. The

status quo is never good enough for Nancy Golden. She believes that everyone can improve, and she has a talent for drawing out the best in others. But most of all, Nancy loves children—all children, especially those who are at risk. It is her passion for meeting the needs of children that has transformed the culture of the entire district and created an environment that attracts talent and allows teacher leadership to flourish. Nancy's work with the S-QEM and "How Are the Children?" can be viewed at www.sps.lane.edu.

REFLECT AND RESPOND

Take a moment to describe the culture of your classroom, school, or community. Knowing that culture must be cultivated, what can you do to improve your corner of the world?

TEACHER LEADERSHIP SCENARIO #2: INSPIRING INSTRUCTIONAL LEADERSHIP

It is the start of a new school year—the first in-service day after a tumultuous season of infighting, bickering, and backstabbing from the year before. Administration at this high school is sick of the juvenile behavior and decides the best way to solve the problem is to allow it to surface. The entire morning is spent griping. Different departments are blaming other departments for bad test scores and supply money shortfalls. It gets so bad that people even start in on blaming each other for parking in designated teacher parking spaces. Everything spoken is negative. The culture is insidious. What can be done? You are a teacher in just such a building. People are drifting. There is no direction. Frustration runs high. The principal doesn't even call staff meetings anymore just to prevent more frustration. Ideas are met with roadblocks. You don't look forward to going to work each day. What do you do?

Think about what you would do and then turn to appendix A: Teacher Leadership Scenario Responses for suggestions about how to respond to the scenario listed above.

3

TEACHER LEADERSHIP ROLES: SCHOOL, DISTRICT, AND PROFESSION

If you want teacher leadership to be successful, you need to create a culture of leadership that emphasizes the importance to everyone. Does the principal encourage teachers to continue their education by setting aside prep time for them to work on their master's degrees? Do teachers share opportunities for professional education? Is administrative staff included in strategy meetings? Is input from everyone who would be affected by a decision included in the decision-making process? Are successes celebrated?

—High School Teacher

STEPPING UP

An eighth-grade middle school science teacher saw a need. Not only were the students in her classes disinterested in the subject she loved, but she also noticed the girls showed a particular lack of engagement in comparison to the boys. She taught in a high-poverty school where more than 70 percent of the students were enrolled in the federal free-and-reduced lunch program. Her students didn't have a lot of experience with science. She tried a variety of classroom experiments to show them how exciting science was, and she always had a good relationship with her students, but it wasn't enough. Then, she got an idea.

She sent special letters of invitation to her students to come after school to join a newly forming science club. Even though all the students got invited, it still made them feel special to get a letter. That first year, 15 of her 180 students expressed interest in spending a little time after school doing some science projects.

She soon found out there was a Science Olympics competition in a neighboring town and got the students in her club interested. They learned about the different categories and requirements for competing in the Olympics. She recruited former high school students as helpers to give the younger students a hand with their projects. She encouraged her most disengaged and disinterested students to participate in the club, and many began taking her up on the offer. For this teacher leader, the club was never about winning a contest—it was about drawing in students and inspiring them about science, education, and life choices.

Year after year, this teacher meets with her students after school to prepare for the Science Olympics, and over time, her students' reputation for excellence has grown. Her students compete for top prizes against schools with far more resources and parent support. The club routinely places in the top three at the state tournament every year. The little club has grown to include nearly 30 percent of her students, and for many of them it is the first time that academics has become meaningful beyond the classroom. Some of her best participants are young girls, and she is inspiring them to become scientists. She does all this year after year without extra pay or fanfare, often spending her own money so her students can have the supplies and equipment they need to compete.

What makes her do it? Why do teachers step into leadership roles when their teaching load is already overwhelming and stressful? For this teacher leader, it is the satisfaction and thrill of seeing students come alive about science. One year, a student confided in her that the only reason she didn't get into a fight with another girl was because she wanted to compete in the Olympics and she knew a fight would result in a suspension from the science club activities. It's that kind of student transformation that motivates and inspires teacher leaders to keep moving forward with their projects and ideas.

Most teachers do not take on the additional stress of formal or informal leadership roles for recognition or salary. The most rewarding leadership roles often go unrecognized and unreimbursed. These gritty leaders simply see a job that needs to be done and embrace the opportunity to step up and make a difference for their students day after day and year after year without flourish or fame.

FORMAL AND INFORMAL LEADERSHIP

There are two kinds of teacher leadership roles: formal and informal. Formal roles are established over time. They are generally recognized positions that teachers sign up for, are recruited to, "volunteer" for, or are assigned. Formal roles include being a department head at a high school, serving on a variety of leadership committees, or being a school or district "instructional coach." Much as already been written (Danielson, 2006; Hasbrouck & Denton, 2005) about formal roles, why they are important, and how teachers can use these roles to improve schools. The purpose of this book is not so much to describe those roles as much as to tell stories about people who have embraced them to make a difference. A degree of authoritative power does comes from formal roles, but authoritative power alone generally does not lend itself to significant improvement in schools. For breakthrough improvement to occur, a degree of relational power has to exist as well.

Informal leadership is all about relational power. Informal leadership occurs when one particular staff member walks into the lunchroom and gets everyone laughing and feeling good about coming to work that day. Informal leadership happens when penetrating questions, the ones that really need to be asked, are asked at a staff meeting before a crucial decision is made. Informal leadership emerges when a thoughtful teacher steps into the principal's office, closes the door, and offers stellar advice. It transpires when a master teacher informally shares curriculum with an inexperienced teacher, or when a new teacher shares what she is learning in her graduate class with her grade-level team. Starting a science club is an outbreak of informal teacher leadership.

Informal leadership happens naturally, but it doesn't happen predictably. It can't be written down in your School Improvement Plan, but it can be seen; when it begins to emerge, how do you respond? Is informal teacher leadership supported in your school and encouraged even though it may be messy, unorganized, and always in need of funding? Principals who support informal teacher leadership wherever and whenever it appears will find their school improving in measurable ways. Understanding the differences between informal and formal teacher leadership helps to differentiate the variety of school, district, and professional leadership roles that exist for teachers. It also helps principals to nurture the seeds of informal leadership when they see them start to sprout, and helps teachers embrace informal and formal leadership opportunities when they become available.

FORMAL SCHOOL ROLES

The educational landscape today is full of many formal opportunities for teachers to demonstrate leadership. Grade-level leaders, department heads, benchmark teams, technology leaders, scheduling and calendar committee leaders, site council representatives, literacy team leaders, behavior support team members, association representation, and instructional support coaches are just a few of the many formal opportunities that are available for teachers at the school level. The literature is rich with explanations of all these roles and their functions, but even more important than job descriptions are the reasons why a teacher is successful in such a role.

Instructional coaching has experienced a resurgence at the school level in recent years. The pressure of yearly testing and accountability has forced schools to examine their practices and make the most efficient decisions that will have the greatest impact for teaching and learning at the classroom level. Even in the midst of classrooms with swelling numbers, many districts have realized that providing an instructional coach at a school can make a bigger, buildingwide impact in student achievement than lowering the teacher-student ratio by one or two children.

One middle school literacy coach found herself in a district that recently made just such a decision. They decided to invest in instructional coaches at every school, and she was the lucky one to step into that role for the first time. What should she do first? How could she be effective? How would the other teachers view her presence? Is there a guidebook somewhere to point the way?

Like many pioneers plunged into these kinds of positions, she was given very little direction, training, or support from the district office for her new role. It was up to her to create it. With the help of a supportive principal, she started small by clearly establishing the fact that she was a teacher leader—not an administrator. Her presence in the classroom was not evaluative. It was supportive, and she made it clear from the beginning she was not a "spy" from the front office. She was there to help, and that was exactly what she set out to do.

She started small by establishing relationships with teachers who were willing to work with her. She observed their classrooms, taught demonstration lessons, and found out what they were interested in. She overcame teachers' natural resistance to outsiders through service. She met needs. Whether it was resources, curriculum ideas, demonstration lessons, teaching their class so they could observe others, or suggestions for hard-to-handle children, she was there.

Every staff is comprised of three kinds of teachers: green zone, yellow zone, and red zone. The green zone teachers get involved with every initiative. They are first to volunteer for committees, take on new projects, or try new ideas. If they are told it's time to take the next hill, they grab their pack and do it—no questions asked.

Yellow zone staff members are different. They come on board if they see success. Generally, they need support and encouragement from a green-zoner to get there.

Red zone teachers make excuses. When told it's time to get their pack and take the next hill, they'll say they don't have a pack. They will only join the movement when critical mass is achieved and they see the train is leaving the station.

Positive teacher leaders operate in the green zone—that's why they are so important to school improvement. When it comes to change agendas, wise principals work with their green and yellow staff to reach critical mass, and they leverage the support of teacher leaders to get there.

Though it is easy in a book to depict entire staffs as having green, yellow, and red participants, individual people are complex. They don't fit into neat little categories, and most people move from zone to zone depending on the topic, work to be done, stage of their life, and sometimes, the time of day. For example, some teachers may be in the green zone when it comes to serving on an attendance committee but in the red zone on the topic of recycling. Individual people can and do change, and system change is dependent on the transformation of individuals. Having a teacher observe and consult your teaching can be very threatening. Many teachers would weigh in on the red zone on that one.

The middle school coach mentioned above became successful in her first school-based coaching assignment because she started with teachers who were in the green zone when it came to instructional coaching, and even though there were just a few, her success with green zone teachers got her invited into the classrooms of teachers who were in the yellow zone. They saw success and wanted to be part of the action.

Red-zoners usually don't jump on the train until they see it start to pull away, and many times they miss the train altogether. Instructional coaching can't be force-fed. There must be a willingness to participate, or it is not effective. That is why coaching models that impose methods or strategies upon everyone are far less successful in generating change than ones that emerge and develop through meeting the authentic needs of teachers and students.

FORMAL DISTRICT ROLES

In January of 1961 a new teacher freshly minted from USC got her first teaching job in a poor community near Watts in Los Angeles. She stepped in midyear to a classroom of 33 kindergarteners in the A.M. and 33 in the P.M. That's right, she saw 66 kindergarteners a day, and when parent conference day arrived, only two parents showed up. In these "good old days" of South Central LA, parental engagement in school was nearly nonexistent. The school itself was huge—warehousing over 1,600 students in grades K–6. The new teacher braved 66 kindergarteners a day in her first year of teaching without any classroom aides or preparation time during the school day. Though times were rough in those thrifty days before Title I funding, the Individuals with Disabilities Act (IDEA), or teacher associations, the district she taught in did have an instructional coach, and an excellent principal went out of his way to ensure that his new teacher would be successful.

The district had grade-level consultants—expert teachers at each grade level whose job was to come in and observe new teachers to provide support, encouragement, and advice. The role of the consultants was not evaluative, and the new teacher was very pleased that someone from the district office was willing to come and observe her on a regular basis to help improve her teaching skills. When it came to coaching, she was in the green zone even though other teachers on her grade-level team told her it was a mistake to let a district consultant into her classroom. She didn't follow their advice and trusted the outsider. She sensed that her principal had her best interests in mind when he suggested she work with the district consultant.

The consultant and new teacher hit it off from day one. The consultant spent many hours in the classroom, recognized the new teacher for things that were going well, and offered helpful suggestions. It didn't take long for the consultant to realize she was working with an exceptional teacher.

Within a year's time, the advice got thinner, and the praise got thicker. Soon the consultant asked if she could bring in some people to observe the classroom. The young teacher had a special talent for keeping 33 kindergarteners busy and on task in two separate sessions throughout each day. Once or twice a month, teachers from around the district would spend an entire morning or afternoon in the classroom. The principal got into the act as well and one time even brought in an entire college classroom to watch. What was her secret? Why was the new teacher so good? She was a natural master at recognizing and supporting positive behavior.

The story of our new teacher demonstrates the priority school officials placed upon district-level instructional coaches more than 45 years ago, at a time when some elementary schools in the inner city didn't even have libraries—including this one in Watts. Flash forward to 2007. Many districts have cut these roles over the years, others have always had them, and some are beginning to recognize the value of instructional coaching and of including them in their staffing plans.

The story also demonstrates the power and connection of formal and informal teacher leadership. Through the consultant's formal role as an instructional coach, she was able to create an opportunity for a new teacher to develop a demonstration class of excellence. Through the many site visits, this teacher's skills and talents came to be emulated by others on an informal level.

All of this was possible because of a principal who believed, supported, and did not feel threatened by teacher leaders. He instinctively knew teaching and learning would improve by supporting instructional coaching in his building, and he worked to find a green zone teacher willing to accept the coaching.

MENTORING PROGRAMS

Over the past few years, Springfield Public Schools in Oregon have developed an extremely effective new teacher mentor program. Like in many districts, administrative leadership in Springfield was distressed by the number of new teachers they were hiring who stayed in the profession less than five years. They recognized that new teachers needed more support than they could get through conventional means.

Having experimented with many different models of support, they came to the realization that the traditional method of assigning a mentor from within the building had many flaws. The full-time teacher had little time or energy to give meaningful support to the new teacher, and the new teachers were often guarded and reticent to talk honestly about their weaknesses, fears, and needs with another teacher in the building. What if those weaknesses got back to the principal somehow? The moment a mentor program becomes evaluative is the moment it becomes ineffective.

What sets Springfield apart is that its mentor program utilizes the expertise of retired teachers. Coordinated by a former Springfield teacher, the program pairs up every new teacher in the district with an outstanding retired educator from Springfield. Mentors are assigned based on teaching expertise and content knowledge. Mentors are assigned to work with teachers in different buildings than they recently retired from. As a result, a safety net of support is created around the new teacher. Mentors meet regularly with the teacher, observe in the classroom, help the new teacher understand how the district functions, and offer curriculum/behavior management advice—in addition to being a friend.

Since the work is so meaningful and has a direct benefit to a new teacher and his or her students, many of the retirees put in extra hours helping and supporting that teacher. Every year, this one-on-one support system helps more than 50 new teachers get grounded in the field and costs less than $40,000 a year. The results in terms of teacher retention and skill improvement are priceless.

INFORMAL ROLES

Informal teacher leadership is the sprocket that powers the chain of school improvement and student achievement. The bigger the gear, the faster you go. However, like riding a bike, you can't start in high gear. Effective informal teacher leadership starts small and builds, but it is through informal leadership that momentum for improvement is created, and it is generally through informal leadership that innovations get introduced into the system.

Since there are so many ways teachers can lead informally, the intent of this section is not to develop a comprehensive list but rather to demonstrate, by way of example, the power of informal teacher leadership to transform schools. Inspiring teachers to seize informal leadership opportunities as they become available is the ultimate goal.

Project-Based Learning

A fifth-grade teacher believed that her students would stay motivated and learn more when the core academic instruction was integrated with engaging topics and culminated in public demonstrations of learning. As a result, she used this type of curriculum design to create a Veteran's Day project that involved students interviewing local war veterans, honoring them with a special dinner, raising money for a local veteran's assistance organization, and conducting a schoolwide assembly so her students could share what they learned with the rest of the school.

Schoolwide Behavior Management

An elementary school's climate committee saw an increase in incidents of disrespect through their monthly reviews of behavior referral data. The committee had a few choices of what to do about it. They could complain to the principal, complain to other staff members, or do something positive to make a difference. One of the teachers decided to make a difference and stepped up as a teacher leader.

Working through the climate committee, she organized a respect assembly that involved the whole school. The committee posted respect signs throughout the school, classrooms wrote songs, and when students saw something that demonstrated respect, they wrote it down. Their goal was to create a student-generated list that showed 100 ways to demonstrate respect, and they far surpassed that goal. A wise teacher leader once said, "You get what you pay attention to," and in this case, the school got respect because that's what they looked for, talked about, and recognized. The entire culture of the school shifted.

Curriculum Development

Many times a new teacher can step into leadership roles through a principal's simple encouragement. A second-year teacher was asked by her principal to participate on a district committee to review the social studies curriculum. She worked alongside another teacher to appraise the scope and sequence of the curriculum and presented her findings to the committee. Through their research, they discovered areas of redundancy in the curriculum, and they brought forth their concerns and proposed a different grade schedule for the social studies curriculum topics. She ended up presenting the proposal with her colleague to the school board. This experience was a huge risk, but one she was willing to take because of the support she had received along the way.

After-School Activities

Teachers can also thrive in leadership roles through nonacademic ways. Being an intramural coordinator was one of the best leadership experiences for one teacher leader because she got to get to know students on a whole new level. It was enlightening to see students who didn't necessarily show strong skills in the classroom become successful in sports, music, art, and a host of other recreational activities. Discovering hidden talents in students and then encouraging students to develop them can be an extremely rewarding experience because it builds positive relationships with students that will carry over to academics in the classroom.

Transition Programs

In an effort to help sixth-graders make a smooth transition to middle school, one teacher took a risk and started a mentoring program that connected eighth- and sixth-graders together. Every year she advocates with administration and convinces teachers this is a project worthy of time and effort. Colleagues remark that if she had not taken those initial risks to try something new and advocate for the program, the school would not have the program today, and it has had a huge impact on the culture of the school in a positive way. Teacher leadership is all about identifying needs, and then rolling up sleeves to tackle those needs—one at a time.

PROFESSIONAL ROLES

Throughout this chapter we have only scratched the surface of traditional and nontraditional leadership roles that exist for teachers. These leadership roles extend far beyond informal and formal opportunities at the school and district levels. Many opportunities to make a difference also exist in other professional organizations.

In Oregon, for example, local associations team up with the State Education Association to set aside a few weekends a year for new teachers to get away from school and share survival stories with experienced teachers. These informal gatherings do a lot for building trust and camaraderie and fighting the feeling of loneliness that many new teachers face in their first few years. The mini-retreats not only provide a time of rest and refreshment for the battle-weary new teachers, but they are also infused with experienced teachers who share their expertise on managing classroom behavior, designing curriculum, and delivering instruction.

Presenting teaching techniques, special programs, and schoolwide reform models at local, state, and national conferences can also be a way for teachers to grow in their leadership skills. Teachers are powerful communicators. When required by the district office to show how his school was making adequate progress on their instructional goals, one smart principal turned the task over to his staff. He knew they would be more convincing than anything he could dream up. When the district accountability team arrived, they were shocked to find out the principal didn't do any of the planning or presenting of the results. It was completely teacher driven. Needless to say, they presented a very convincing tale about the school's effectiveness, and the district office team left highly impressed.

REFLECT AND RESPOND

Brainstorm all of the formal and informal leadership roles that exist in your school, district, and profession. What roles would you like to play? What can you do today to get started? In what ways are you a green, yellow, or red zone teacher? How about your colleagues? Think about a teacher who was ineffective in a leadership role. Being able to avoid negative examples is just as important as following positive ones. What made that person ineffective? Was their role formal or informal? What could they have done to improve?

TEACHER LEADERSHIP SCENARIO #3: PRINCIPAL PETS

It seems like the principal has some "pets" or "favorites" on the staff, and you are not one of them—nor do you want to be. However, you want to have a leadership role in the school, but all of the leadership roles are going to the favorites. You have a good relationship with the superintendent because your district is not very big, and she is very visible in the schools and community, but you don't want to tell the superintendent because you're worried that she'll tell the principal and then things will get worse. What do you do?

Think about what you would do and then turn to appendix A: Teacher Leadership Scenario Responses for suggestions about how to respond to the scenario listed above.

4

FROM THE PRINCIPAL'S OFFICE:
HOW TO SUPPORT TEACHERS
IN LEADERSHIP ROLES

> Listening, learning, and leading are three points of a trian-
> gle. If one crumbles, the rest are sure to follow. You cannot
> have one without the other. Good leaders listen to others.
> It is not always a sit-down meeting where troubles are dis-
> cussed, however. Leaders listen when others aren't directly
> talking to them. Leaders seek out the issues and learn how
> to solve them by listening to others. If they did everything
> on their own, then they wouldn't be great leaders.
>
> —Elementary School Teacher

Supporting teacher leadership from the principal's office is a priority
for every effective leader. There is no comprehensive training program for developing teacher leaders. Teacher leadership is organic, not
prescriptive. It develops and grows when the conditions are right. The
key to increasing teacher leadership in your school is to continually create and re-create the right conditions. In this way, the development of
teacher leaders can be intentional, and it will be achieved when administrators engage in the following practices: (1) authentic listening,
(2) recognition and support, and (3) active risk taking.

PRINCIPAL PRACTICE #1:
EMPLOY AUTHENTIC LISTENING

I think leading implies that you are representing someone else and are
becoming someone else's voice. It is impossible to represent someone
unless you are authentically listening. For others to support their

43

leader, they need reassurance that their leader has taken the time to connect with them and their concerns. After listening to their needs, it is the leader's job to learn all he or she can to advocate for the needs that his or her supporters described. Absolutely, leaders need to first be listeners. Otherwise, it would become very tempting to think of one's own agenda, which would make it difficult to authentically listen to any other perspectives, complicating one's ability to work well with others. (Elementary School Teacher)

Effective leaders listen. Leading is a by-product of learning, and learning comes from listening. People, in general, don't listen very well. Some listen so they can be heard, but few listen with the intent to be changed. In the majority of conversations, people listen so they can formulate their own ideas and then speak to communicate them. Very few individuals authentically listen to others to the point where there is no hidden agenda, no convincing going on in the background.

Principals who are trying to inspire leadership around them must practice the art of authentic listening (Hess and Robinson, 2006). They must be willing to leave their own agenda at the door and welcome the ideas and thoughts of others. When teachers see and understand that their principal is not just hearing them but is also responding to what they are saying by making course corrections, they will begin to walk with confidence that they can be agents of change. They will intuitively know they can be leaders.

A high school was required to alter its school schedule in order to create more credit opportunities for students. A team of ten teachers and the principal were wrestling with this dilemma for several months, and in the end the team provided four possible models to the rest of the staff. None of the models was a clear-cut favorite. Other teachers begin bringing forward alternative ideas. Soon a schedule that was completely different from the others was brought to the team and eventually made it to a staff vote. The staff overwhelmingly supported the alternative option.

It would have been very easy for that principal to turn down ideas that didn't originate with him or with the group that was assigned to investigate the scheduling options. It would have been even quicker—but not easier—for the district office to send down the "proper" schedule from downtown, but either scenario would not have fostered teacher leadership.

In the end, the teachers chose the schedule that would require the most work on their part. To implement their preference, they would have to revamp the entire curriculum and learn how to teach in longer blocks of time, but they were willing to do the work and engage in deep change because someone was smart enough not only to listen but also to act upon what he heard.

During my tenure as a principal, one of the ongoing challenges was the creation of a report card that accurately reflected what students knew and could do at the various levels of the system. Over a six-year period, my district at the time designed a continuous progress model of education to be implemented in grades K–8. In this model, social promotion and retention were rejected. Social promotion was defined as sending students on to the next grade level without the academic skills they needed to be successful, and retention was defined as repeating the same unsuccessful treatment again. Research and experience tell us both practices are not good for students. Our continuous progress model and its successes are documented in the book *Excellence, Equity, Efficiency* (Hess, 2005).

The problem with our reporting system was clear. What we were doing with the report card was always a few paces behind the innovations of the system, and even though the district developed a K–12 learning continuum that reflected our continuous progress model, at my school we weren't pleased with the amount of detail and information we needed to report to parents at each level. In the age of automation, we were searching for something meaningful, authentic, and relevant. Our biggest obstacle was time. We just couldn't find the time to sit down in groups to develop something that reflected our best thinking.

Then, out of the blue, my two first-grade teachers helped all of us stop admiring the problem. They came to me on a Friday, desperately wanting to change the report card to make it more meaningful for parents, and handed me two pages of scribbled-out notes and cross-outs from other report cards plus some ideas of their own. They sheepishly asked if I could create a report card from their ideas.

My first reaction was, "Do it yourself. I don't have the time," which, of course, was true. I didn't have any time. My second reaction was, "I can't make any changes because the district office would have to approve them first." That was not true. Our district office was constantly encouraging dissidence and deviation from the norm because the leadership recognized and knew that innovation and improvement don't happen when people only do what they are told.

I was tempted to share the second reaction. It is easy and believable to blame the district office, state department, or federal government for why things can't be done. I could have easily hammered down the district office's reputation and built mine by not providing the real reason for not wanting to change the report card—my lack of time and their lack of computer expertise.

Then I thought of a third reaction, which was a combination of the first two: "There's not enough time to do it for this report card. Let's work on it for the year so we can get it approved by the district." This third option would be a stall tactic. We'd already been putting off changing the report card for over a year, and my years in school have taught me that there will never be enough time—the pace of work will never slow down—and if we use that as an excuse for our inaction, things will never improve. It's important to realize, of course, that all of these thoughts blazed through my brain while the two teachers were standing in my doorway awaiting an answer. I think they could tell I was wrestling with how to respond.

I cycled through all the possibilities, and then chose to support teacher leadership—even though it would cost me a great deal of time and energy. I had been encouraging report card transformation for over a year, and now I finally had a couple of brave teachers who took me up on the challenge. They only needed my help and support to make it happen. Authentic listening often leads to action. I also had a hunch that if I took their ideas and put them into a readable form on the computer, other teachers would want similar effective redesigns for their levels. By empowering them to choose the content, I was developing their leadership skills. They just needed a little service to get it done.

I appreciated the fact that these teachers put their energy into innovation and improvement. I wanted to encourage that behavior whenever and wherever I saw it, but I was pressed for time. Early in my administrative career I learned a key motto when working with people that has kept me out of many jams: underpromise and overdeliver. Don't tell people you can do something just to make them happy. Intentionally lower their initial expectations by underpromising. Then, as you are able, step up and deliver beyond their expectations. Practicing that principle over time builds trust and confidence in your leadership, and you will not only develop a reputation for exceeding the expectations of others but work hard to keep it. I told my first-grade teachers I would do what I could and get back to them.

I knew taking on this job would be several hours of work on my computer at home, but if I truly believed in teacher leadership, if I truly wanted a new and improved reporting system that teachers owned and parents appreciated, I needed to help. Principals and other administrators are key supporters of teacher leadership. We must be willing to encourage innovation and know when to step in to make it a reality. We all need support to improve.

I got busy with the report card redesign based upon their ideas. When I finished a weekend later, the two teachers liked what they saw. It not only fulfilled their needs, but I added some key elements I had been encouraging as well. It didn't take long for the word to spread. "Did you see what first grade came up with for the report card? I want one!" It worked. Good ideas spread. They take off and leadership spreads as a result. Soon the rest of the grade- and benchmark-level teams were coming to me with ideas. Since I had already redesigned the first-grade level, it wasn't hard to do the rest. Within a few months—without months of planning meetings to admire the problem—we had a comprehensive reporting system that communicated to parents not only what their child knew and was able to do but also included the goals and expectations for the next level of achievement as well.

PERCEPTION IS NOT REALITY

The problem with authentically listening is that most of the time principals do not perceive themselves as others perceive them. In a recent Metlife Survey (2003) that asked a variety of questions from principals, teachers, and parents at the same school, more than half of the principals surveyed (53 percent) rated themselves as excellent listeners, compared to only one in three teachers (30 percent) and parents (27 percent). Lesson learned: The person doing the listening is not highly qualified to judge whether or not he or she is a good listener.

One teacher leader tells the story of her principal who began the school year with an open-door policy, but as the year wore on, the stacks of paperwork grew higher and that door was closed more often than not. The message communicated to staff was clear, "My work is important. I can't be disturbed." However, this same principal would stop in and interrupt a teacher if the occasion arose and wouldn't think twice about it. The atmosphere created over time was very authoritative, and it communicated that the one at the top was deserving of respect, but those below were not. Needless to say, the principal who does not make herself available to others is by default a poor listener, and she's not likely to be inspiring informal teacher leadership.

Anonymous surveys are one way to get unbiased data about your ability to listen, but reflecting on how you spent your day might be even more telling. How much time do you spend in your office versus in classrooms or out on supervision? Being visible around the school is a very effective way to listen. When you are out of your office, you are listening with your eyes. You are learning about what is happening on the playground, in classrooms, and in the lunchroom. By stepping out of your office, you are making a conscious choice to set aside your agenda—all of the paperwork demanding your attention—and listen to what is happening in your school. Effective leaders make that choice often, and when they are making their rounds, they learn new things, observe new behaviors, and change in the process. They become smarter. Another way to take your listening temperature is to think about how much time you spend asking questions versus telling people things. Leaders who ask questions end up being effective and authentic listeners.

The same lessons apply to the classroom as well. If you are a teacher, ask yourself whether or not you do an excellent job of listening to your students. Then ask your students the same question. Allow them to write their answer and a reason for their answer. There is a good chance your students don't feel like you listen to them as much as you feel like you do, but remember, the leader laws apply universally. If you want your students to become leaders, then start by authentically listening to them. Listen with the intent to be changed.

The leaders whom I have respected the most and have worked the hardest for have been people who I would consider authentic listeners.

The current principal in my building is a very active and reflective listener. He has a very open communication style that enables anyone who steps into his office to receive his full attention, free of judgment or his own personal agenda. And the leaders whom I have had the most conflict with were people with whom I never felt truly comfortable or respected in conversations. I certainly never saw a door open to bring in my concerns and challenges, let alone an empathetic ear or heart. (Elementary Teacher)

THE POWER OF LEARNING TEAMS

Having teachers work in teams is an effective way to foster and practice authentic listening. High-achieving schools are filled with teachers who have learned how to "listen" to their data through questions and reflection. Teachers have been working together in buildings for decades, but it has only been in the last few years that we have begun to realize the influence of effective data teams on school improvement.

The recent work around Professional Learning Communities (Dufour & Eaker, 1998) is helping to define and attach code words to the work high-achieving schools have been doing all along. To help us move beyond jargon, the bedrock of Professional Learning Communities (PLCs) is teams of staff members who engage in the following behaviors (Robbins, 2005):

- They are dedicated to the goal of helping all students succeed and envision themselves as lifelong learners.
- They meet regularly to engage in collective inquiry, problem solving, and reflection about teaching and learning.
- They focus on studying data and working together to grow professionally.
- They focus on building a collaborative, student-focused culture to improve outcomes for all students.

Effective PLCs require more than drive-by workshops. PLCs are learning teams committed to ongoing inquiry, designing interventions based on their inquiry, implementing the interventions, and then measuring the results, but teachers need time to engage in this meaningful work if they are to develop as teacher leaders and learn how to listen to what the data is telling them.

Even though the term "PLC" is mostly the regifting of the work on quality circles and learning teams, that is no reason to discard the movement. The concept of inquiry circles around data goes back to Shewart's PDSA (Plan, Do, Study, Act) cycle in the 1930s, and organizations committed to quality improvement have been doing it ever since (Deming, 1986; Senge, 1994; Bonstingl, 2001). The issue isn't that schools do not know what to do; it's just that many are not doing it. Figure 4.1 is a simple graphic that visually depicts the essential work of teams that learn. As the figure illustrates, learning teams deeply engage in the following activities on a regular basis:

- Ask questions
- Analyze the answers
- Design interventions based upon the analysis
- Implement interventions based upon the design
- Measure the result of their implementations

Asking questions is the vehicle for generating data. Too often in education we get binders of data tossed our way from the district office or state department, and we have very little time to analyze and reflect on that data. We rarely even begin to ask meaningful questions about it. However, the answers always lie in the questions. Effective learning teams are inquisitive. Staffed by teacher leaders, they dig deep into the data, asking questions every step of the way in order to get a greater understanding of the problem so that they can design an intervention that will address the core issue rather than surface ones. This is the heart of systemic change.

There is a catch, however. A team of teachers that does not believe all children can achieve at high levels is not a learning team, and all of the books, workshops, charts, and how-to lists will never amount to anything more than rearranging the deck chairs on the *Titanic*. The foundation of the work on continuous improvement is the core belief that all children can learn and achieve. If this foundation is not laid and regularly emphasized in a thousand ways—beginning with the principal—then the PLC teams in your school will never be effective, and the movement will end up as just another set of clothes in the emperor's closet.

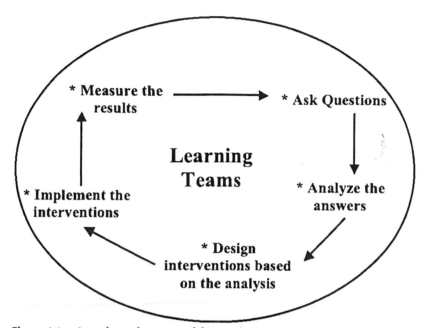

Figure 4.1. In order to be successful, Learning Teams must believe all students can learn and achieve at high levels. The cycle of learning begins with asking questions. Questions generate data. Analysis of the data leads to interventions. Implementing interventions provides results. Results must be measured, which leads to more questions. . . .

In conclusion, authentic listening is the match that ignites leadership in those around you, and the key to becoming an authentic listener is really very simple: Be visible, ask questions, and respond to what you learn. Talk less. Do more. Be inquisitive. Through this process, you will begin to see leadership emerge all around you, and as sparks fly and flames begin to form, the next crucial step will be to keep those flames fed.

PRINCIPAL PRACTICE #2:
RECOGNITION AND SUPPORT

If you are a principal, teacher leadership is occurring all around you—formally and informally. Stop and think about it. We get what we pay attention to. If you recognize and support the teacher leadership that already exists in your school, you will see more and more of it occurring over time.

Many times we fall into the trap of paying too much attention to staff members who are complaining or are unhappy in some way. There is a tendency to try "not to upset them." When we operate in that kind of fear-based environment, we end up stifling the embers of any teacher leadership that does exist. When our attention and energy goes toward pacifying people who do not operate in possibility, we send a clear message to those who do—you are not important.

If we publicly recognize those who have stepped into leadership roles—even small ones—we send the message that teachers will be recognized for behaving like leaders. Over time, such recognition will help more and more teachers to take on leadership roles. On the other hand, constantly giving voice to disagreeable people will eventually make everyone disagreeable.

FIND THE EXPERTS

In the brief span of three years, a large comprehensive high school skyrocketed from the bottom five on the tenth-grade state math assessment to the top five. It was an incredible turnaround and curriculum leaders from around the state gathered to examine just how it happened. It is not easy to pinpoint effective systemic change because it isn't linear or predictable. They did not find a newly implemented math curriculum, piles of extra resources, or cheating, but they did find several teachers who had not been satisfied with the status quo. Somewhere along the line they stopped making excuses and were willing to do something different. Change usually begins when someone, somewhere, stops making excuses, stops the shame-and-blame game, and simply declares that things just need to get better.

In addition to teachers willing to change, they also found at the heart of the reform a teacher who became an expert at understanding the content of the state test. Given some release time to work with other teachers, develop common assessments, and redesign the math curriculum so that it thoroughly covered the testable content, this teacher leader was able to help the entire department improve what was taught and when it was taught. The improvement was truly a team effort with everyone playing a part, but kneeling in the middle of the huddle directing the action was a leader—a teacher who was given the time and resources to become an expert in her field.

For nearly 30 years, an outstanding teacher worked in near obscurity at the fourth- and fifth-grade levels. Over time he developed a deep knowledge of the curriculum, and an uncanny ability to reach out and connect with the neediest children in the room. He was a bona fide, unrecognized expert. He was unrecognized because he didn't draw attention to himself. He was quiet in staff meetings except for the occasional thoughtful question. Every year his students excelled on state tests to such a degree that rumors surfaced of cheating. In his last year, his students were removed from the room for the writing assessment "just to be safe." Guess what? They outperformed the rest of the district that year too.

This teacher believed that students learned best if they could understand patterns or steps to accomplishing complex tasks, and he used his theory to teach everything from writing to math problem solving. He relentlessly trained students—especially the most at risk—to memorize, understand, and apply the patterns. His tenacity paid off again and again and again for hundreds of students down through the years. Perhaps everyone would have benefited more if they could have learned from his expertise rather than doubt his unorthodox, "old school" methods.

The story has a happy ending. Upon retirement, this unheralded teacher became a writing coach at several Title I schools where 70 percent to 90 percent of the students were on free and reduced lunch and many were in need of second-language services. These schools embraced his methods and saw results that outperformed other schools in and out of their socioeconomic range as well.

Identifying experts is critical to the emergence of teacher leaders, and many times those experts are not conventional people. Every staff has teachers who are known for specific craft knowledge; however, most teachers—especially the good ones—do not spend much time tooting their own horns. They need to be recognized. They are in the service industry, not sales. As a result, some structured activities may be needed for teachers to begin sharing their expertise with others. In order to allow the talent in your staff to surface, try the following activity.

STAFF ACTIVITY: NOMINATE THE EXPERTS

Pass out numbered 3×5 index cards to everyone in the room. Have each teacher write down or remember the number on his or her card. On one side of the card, have each person write down one specific teaching skill area in which he or she would like to improve. It could be classroom management, teaching a particular concept, unit ideas, technology needs, PE activities, writing strategies, homework motivation ideas, free-time games, service learning projects, recess line-up, literacy strategies, grading techniques, field trip ideas, or anything else they would like some support with. Pass around the cards and give each person 30 seconds to write down on the back of the card the name of someone in the room who has craft knowledge in that area and might be able to help them.

If someone can't think of a person to nominate, they leave that card blank. Once the cards have been around the room several times, each person gets his or her original card back by recalling their number. All of the people with even numbers have 30 seconds to find someone in the room who has been named on their card as having some skill or expertise on their requested topic. Give staff three to five minutes to pick their brain for some ideas. Then have odd numbers do the same thing.

After a few rounds of each person having an opportunity to talk to someone about his or her need, debrief the activity with the group. What did people learn? How did it feel to have someone ask you about something you do well? How did it feel to be recognized by your peers? Practice authentic listening when sharing in this activity by listening with the intent to be changed. Try to improve your practice in some specific way.

Notice how this teacher leader facilitates listening to others by deliberately seeking out advice from peers:

> I take time out of my schedule to seek out others to build relationships. Too often teachers tend to stay in our areas only. I have to work after hours anyway, and the 10 or 15 minutes I take for a colleague can help both of us more than the time in my room. I also ask a lot of questions, trying to draw people out of themselves to help me clarify my thinking and get new perspectives. I also meet regularly with a couple for collaboration. Math is a huge issue in the classes I

teach, and the math teacher and I have worked on some of the concepts and presentations together. (Middle School Teacher)

PRINCIPAL PRACTICE #3: ACTIVE RISK TAKING

Comfort zones are easy to stay in, and administration can make all the difference in the world. I also think that sometimes if the administration is not aware that risks need to be taken and does nothing to encourage it, comfort zones come into play. Some teachers aren't even aware that they are in a comfort zone. They don't even know there are risks to be taken. They think that teaching is only in the classroom and they get off at 4:00. The administration not only needs to be a safety strap but an encourager as well. I know at my old school, my principal asked me to do things that required risks. Now, I am asked to do nothing and I have to actually make it a point to take my own risks. It would be very easy for me to never come out of my classroom shell. (Elementary Teacher)

An elementary teacher and a middle school teacher were experimenting with new levels of technology in their classrooms. This technology included a variety of innovative practices including digital portfolios, advanced PowerPoint use, webquests, and webpage design. Encouraged by the district technology director, these teachers conducted after-school drop-in training for other teachers in the district. Teachers were compensated for their time, and because teachers who were learning themselves led the sessions, the instruction was extremely relevant to their needs. Teachers were able to bring their own technology projects and needs to the training so they received just-in-time embedded professional development.

Our two innovative teachers would never consider themselves technology experts, and it was risky for them to step up and lead the training. The only missing ingredient for teacher leadership to emerge in this case was some encouragement and an opportunity. The district technology director provided both, and the end result was improved technology skills for teachers and increased learning opportunities for students.

Leadership does not occur without risk taking, and when teachers know that their principal and other supervisors will be supportive of risk taking rather than critical, they are much more likely to take on leadership roles.

> Teacher leadership involves taking risks. It involves being aware of situations occurring in education and advocating for best practices in one's own classroom and throughout the school and school district. It also includes being able to support other staff members as they venture into the unknown and begin to take risks themselves. (Elementary Teacher)

STAFF ACTIVITY: BUILD CONFIDENCE THROUGH CRAFT KNOWLEDGE

Start the meeting by sharing that your purpose is to increase teacher confidence by recognizing specific expert craft knowledge among the staff. On separate 4×6 index cards, write down the names of all your staff members. Randomly pass the cards out to the meeting participants. This activity will work best in a group of 15 to 25 people. Let everyone know they will have 30 seconds to write a specific strength on each person's card. Pass the cards every 30 seconds. When the cards come to you, write a new strength you have noticed or put a check by one that is already written down.

This is a silent activity. When the time is done, return each card to the person whose name is on it. This activity will build confidence in your staff, and having the courage to step out and be willing to take risks is crucial when it comes to developing teacher leaders. Conclude the activity by going around the room and having each person briefly share a craft knowledge strength that others have noticed, and how they were able to develop that strength.

THE POWER OF SAFETY STRAPS

In *Learning by Heart* (2001), author and reformer Roland Barth writes about the importance and necessity of a harness, or safety strap, when scaling mountains. For many teachers, pursuing leadership opportunities is like scaling mountains, and they are not likely to attempt it unless they know they are anchored somewhere. Building confidence between staff members is the best kind of safety strap, and it can be done in a variety of ways.

In my first middle school principalship, I took the entire staff to an off-site ropes course where we learned and grew together with actual safety straps. We had low-impact and high-impact experiences while climbing, thinking, and solving problems together. We learned about each other and bonded more in that one day of training than we would have sitting through a week's worth of school in-services in the library. There is something powerful about experience-based learning, and it can be a tremendous way to build the confidence necessary to scale the mountain of teacher leadership.

CONFIDENCE THROUGH MISTAKES

Your willingness to admit mistakes can be a big confidence builder for staff members. When an acrobat stumbles on the high wire, what does he do? He throws up his hands and everyone applauds. The acrobat is, in effect, stating, "I messed up. Clap for me. Build my confidence." In education we are quick to point fingers and place blame. We need to get better at admitting our mistakes, taking a round of applause, and moving on. The applause is not for a job well done. The applause is a way of saying, "Keep trying. Don't give up. I believe in you."

Mistakes by leaders are obvious to all. Hiding them only makes matters worse. Effective leaders develop protocols for admitting mistakes and model mistake-owning behavior. Whether it is throwing up your hands and asking for a round of applause or some other protocol, your acknowledgment of imperfection lets staff members know they can take a risk, make a mistake, and not be punished or ridiculed for it.

Being able to admit and own mistakes is the first healthy step toward change and improvement. Schools are places steeped in tradition, and it is not easy to move them—or try new methods—when there is a feeling that the new method is just another "fad" that will come and go. Education has a long history of bandwagon-jumping and front-running. However, when people have the courage—and wisdom—to admit their mistakes, the walls come down just a little bit. People are a little less defensive, and have a little more confidence to change and try another innovation that just might make the difference.

Theodore Roosevelt once said, "It is common sense to take a method and try it. If it fails, admit it frankly and try another. But above all, try something." Teddy's words ring just as true today as they did 100 years ago. Yes, indeed, don't let fear of failure prevent you from trying something.

REFLECT AND RESPOND

Describe how informal and formal teacher leadership is currently occurring in your school. What can you do to recognize and support that teacher leadership? How can you practice authentic listening? Take a look at figure 4.1. How deeply have you implemented the core practices of learning teams in your school? Does your staff believe that all children can learn and achieve at high levels?

TEACHER LEADERSHIP SCENARIO #4: TEAM CONFLICT

You are the principal and there is conflict on one of your grade-level teams. Some of the teachers are having a hard time getting along. There is a lot of backbiting and gossip, and the team doesn't seem to be making much progress as a group. They are not systematically looking at data, designing interventions, or implementing them. The only thing they are doing is meeting together—sporadically. The culture of the group is poor as well. You recognize the problem, but don't really want to get involved because you are trying to keep your involvement on grade-level teams at a minimum. You would like the team leader to step in and do something to improve how the team functions, but he thinks it is not that big of a deal and would like to avoid any conflict or telling his colleagues what to do. Unfortunately, the situation seems to be getting worse, not better. What do you do?

Think about what you would do and then turn to appendix A: Teacher Leadership Scenario Responses for suggestions about how to respond to the scenario listed above.

5

SUPPORTING TEACHER LEADERSHIP THROUGH PROFESSIONAL DEVELOPMENT

Anything worth doing is worth doing badly at first.

—Elementary Teacher

A few years ago, a statewide literacy conference had all of the high fliers in attendance. There were big university researchers, authors of dynamic reading programs, and a host of other staff developers. At the keynote address, the woman who won Teacher of the Year got up to address the crowd and said simply, "I am not really sure why they wanted me to speak with you all today. I don't have a fancy degree from a prestigious university. I haven't served on national committees, reviewed all of the reading programs out there, or written a book. The only thing I've done is taught over 1,000 children how to read." The crowd of practitioners stood up and cheered. Teaching is hard, complex work, and when it comes to professional development, teachers prefer to hear from someone who has done it or is doing it.

URBAN LEGEND

ABC High School was heard to have blown the doors off student achievement. The school was the highest-performing school in the state. They received visitors from all around trying to understand how they got so good. Eventually, word of their success reached The University. Even though The University didn't fund research at this school or sponsor the reform that was occurring, they sent a Professor as a representative just to see what was happening.

The Professor spent a day at the school and discovered, sure enough, a lot of good things were occurring at ABC High School. The students were engaged. The curriculum was relevant, and the standards were rigorous. Teachers discussed student work in the hallways, and the faculty room was full of data charts on student achievement. A culture of accountability, learning, and achievement could be observed everywhere.

At the end of the day, The Professor summoned the staff together to review his findings and opened the meeting by remarking, "Good things are happening here at ABC High School. Test scores are up. Achievement is at an all-time high. Your reform is working in practice. Now, you are ready for the next step. I will take what you are doing back to The University to see if it will work in theory."

NEW CONCEPT: TEACHERS
AND PRINCIPALS AS EXPERTS

Although the urban legend mentioned above seems a little far-fetched, practitioners are constantly faced with the reality of dealing with experts on schooling who don't work in schools. Education is full of consultants. Those consultants offer professional development, and they are deemed to be "the experts." They approve of what works and disapprove of what does not work. In theory, they are the ultimate authority and decide what is "best practice." Many times these "experts" are university professors, central office administrators, or staff developers who have spent very little time in a classroom as a K–12 teacher, but somehow they know what is "best for students," and we keep letting them tell us. How did this happen?

When teachers and principals allow theory to trump practice, we hand over the keys to the kingdom. We lose our ability to lead. Practice should inform theory. Edward Deming, the founder of the quality movement and the notion of continuous improvement, emphasized that the people closest to the work know the most about the work, and smart organizations learn how to tap that reservoir of expertise. Teachers are the practitioners, and their ideas should not only be highly valued but also diligently sought out. Principals work closely with teachers, and their voice is critical in helping to establish teachers as leaders in our profession.

PROFESSIONAL DEVELOPMENT
FOSTERS TEACHER LEADERSHIP

Providing high-quality training for teachers is absolutely essential for teacher leadership to flourish. Teachers step into leadership roles when they begin to realize they have something valuable to share with others, and many times they discover those treasures by sharing with other teachers the knowledge and skills they have learned through training or practice. One of the most frustrating things in public education is the lack of value we place on professional development.

When budgets are tight, professional development for teachers is often the first thing to go. The public—and even school leaders—somehow see training as a fringe benefit, something "extra," and the "real work" is being with students all day. The truth of the matter is that ineffective teaching is little more than babysitting, and teachers rarely become effective without high-quality training.

In the 21st century we don't need a research study to tell us that high-quality staff development must be job-embedded, ongoing, and relevant to be effective. We know that already, but that kind of training is a lot easier to say than to deliver. Effective training changes practice, but most staff development falls short because the ideas contained in the handouts never make it from the training room to the classroom.

One of the most effective models of professional development I've seen involves trainers actually going into classrooms and providing demonstration lessons while the teacher observes what is occurring and then attempts to re-create what was modeled. This kind of "on the field" coaching for excellence is what is meant by "job-embedded professional development."

Whether the goal is to incorporate technology, introduce a new method to teach writing, demonstrate reading strategies, or implement a new reading adoption, "just-in-time" professional development that occurs with real students and the teacher who is being trained is by far the most effective way to learn new skills. It is also the most expensive because it involves having coaches on site or paid trainers who visit classrooms. Districts that have invested in this model and are implementing it effectively are seeing immediate results in the classroom.

STAFF ACTIVITY: THE BEST OF
TIMES AND THE WORST OF TIMES

In this activity, teachers share effective and ineffective professional development experiences they have encountered throughout their careers in education. Structure the group in a circle so that sharing can be maximized between staff members. Begin by announcing that the purpose of the meeting is to share the most effective and least effective professional development experiences people have had during their careers. Pass out a sheet of paper that states "best" on one side and "worst" on the other. Give staff five to ten minutes to jot down some reflective thoughts about the best and worst professional development they have experienced. Encourage them to record stories and experiences rather than simply what went wrong or right with the training.

After everyone has had a few minutes to think and jot some things down, begin the conversation by having staff members share their worst experiences. Encourage them to keep their stories short, around three minutes each. Staff can commiserate with the experiences, but try to keep the activity moving forward by not delving too deeply into any one story. While people are sharing, capture the key features of each bad experience on chart paper in the front of the room. For instance, if someone had a bad experience with a training that was not what they needed or were interested in, write down "irrelevant." After around 20 minutes of sharing, you will have started a nice list of things to avoid when it comes to professional development for teachers.

Shift the conversation by having staff now focus on professional development that was meaningful and effective—the best experiences. Use a similar process of allowing staff members to share their experiences. Continue to capture the unique features of the quality training on another piece of chart paper. Allow a little more time for people to share their good experiences and stories. As the sharing continues, you will notice the energy in the room picking up. Good stories do that.

When you are finished with this activity, staff members will not only know each other a little better, but you will also find out what kind of trainings they have been exposed to, how effective those trainings were, what you should avoid when designing staff development, and who the future leaders of the group might be based on the training they have had; you will also have set a standard for effective professional development in your school.

UNIVERSAL LITERACY STRATEGIES

The most comprehensive model of professional development for emergent teacher leaders has a three-pronged attack: (1) universal literacy strategies across the content areas, (2) subject-specific content strategies, and (3) skills for success that benefit all teachers.

It is beyond dispute that reading is the gateway academic skill. Students who do not master reading skills in school have increasingly limited opportunities beyond school. We used to believe that reading was taught to children when they were young, and as they progressed through school, there was no longer a need to teach reading skills—we just needed to provide students with opportunities to read. We know better now.

We are beginning to understand that students need to be taught reading strategies throughout their school career, and that these reading strategies are the very skills they will need to access the complex and challenging texts they will encounter in science, social studies, and government classes as they continue their education. Any teacher who puts words in front of children in the form of textbooks needs to be able to help those students access text through effective reading strategies.

Teachers can get ideas about ways to support reading through books, conferences, and staff development, but in order to change practice, most teachers need to see how these strategies work with teachers in real classrooms to understand how to implement them.

Reading Apprentice (RA) is a program designed to teach students to think about what they read. Districts across the country have begun to implement the concepts of RA. Reading Apprentice is not a canned reading program, but a collection of tools where teachers are deeply trained how to use a variety of reading strategies that are designed to help students to comprehend texts in depth.

More information about RA can be found at www.wested.org. The best-selling book *Reading for Understanding* (Schoenbach, Greenleaf, Cziko, & Hurwitz, 2000) highlights many of the concepts used in the training. The program is designed especially for content teachers in grades 6–12, but the strategies can be helpful in intermediate (fourth and fifth) grades as well.

Universal literacy for learning is the ultimate goal of a K–12 education. Literacy begins with reading and is supported by writing. A strong body of research supports the importance of teaching writing—especially nonfiction writing—across the curriculum (Reeves, 2006). Staffs that systemically teach writing and collaboratively score writing samples in all disciplines outperform schools that do not emphasize writing—and not just in writing. They also outperform other schools in math, science, and reading as well. Without question, an effective staff development program must start with universal literacy for all teachers.

LEXILES FOR LITERACY

Harnessed by the power of teacher leaders, Springfield Public Schools was able to boost universal literacy training across the district by developing a Lexile team. Lexiles are a scientific and accurate way to measure the readability of any text. The Lexile readability formula is derived by combining the words used in a sentence (more common words are worth fewer points) and the length of sentences (longer sentences are worth more points). Equipped with the technology to scan entire books, Lexiles are based upon the entire document to be scanned and are far more accurate than the traditional grade-level ratings. Lexile resources can be found and are explained in their entirety at www.lexile.com.

The Lexile team in Springfield is composed of teachers trained in how to use Lexile information to help teachers find materials students can read independently at their level so that they are not frustrated. Because most major textbooks are equipped with Lexile ratings, teachers who are aware of the Lexile range of their students are able to more effectively meet the reading needs of their students and can provide additional reading instruction to students who need more support to access difficult texts.

SUBJECT-SPECIFIC TRAINING

In addition to literacy training that helps all students read and write across the content areas, it is also important for districts to have subject-specific professional development that taps the expertise of teacher leaders throughout the district. Social studies, math, science, PE, fine arts, health, foreign language, English-language learner (ELL), special education, counselors, and other subject-specific teachers need ongoing training that is targeted to district priorities and teacher needs and interests. These trainings should be coordinated at a district level so that there is ongoing support and systemic direction.

In tight budget times, some districts try to support these teachers through specific grants that help teachers learn in-depth content knowledge and strategies for communicating key content, but even when grant funds are not available, it is critically important to provide teachers with opportunities to meet and share with each other curriculum and instructional ideas and strategies. Every school and district has people in these areas who have key craft knowledge, but without giving them an opportunity to share with their peers, we are missing huge opportunities for professional development and teacher leader growth.

In their book *Saving Our Students, Saving Our Schools* (2003), Barr and Parrett write about several effective strategies high-poverty districts are using to achieve breakthrough results, and many of the strategies are commonsense ones like the large school district that analyzed its highest-performing classrooms at the fifth-grade level across the district on the state test in math and simply invited those teachers together for a summer workshop to share lesson plans and learn from each other. The project resulted in a "best of the best" instructional notebook that was published for others to use in their classrooms. The hard work of these teachers was validated through the process, and many of them had a confidence boost that enabled them to develop into teacher leaders back in their respective buildings.

UNIVERSAL SKILLS AND TRAINING

Beyond literacy for learning and subject-specific training, districts committed to developing highly trained leader teachers also have a plan for delivering universal training and skills to their staffs—including classified staffs. One of the most profoundly transforming universal trainings that has the potential to renovate entire school cultures is Positive Behavior

Support (PBS). Outlined in the book *Best Behavior* (Golly & Sprague, 2005), entire staffs, including classified personnel, are trained to have the same behavior expectations throughout all domains of the school. Using recognition systems to encourage students to follow schoolwide expectations and ongoing training to instruct students about the expectations, PBS schools can reduce office referrals by 50 percent within one year.

Classroom management strategies, cooperative learning, character education, and teacher evaluation systems are just a few of the many other types of universal trainings that all teachers can benefit from. Making sure these types of trainings are research-based, coordinated efforts is critical if a district is going to avoid being accused of an uncoordinated smattering of staff development efforts. In these days of NCLB accountability, most districts must develop some kind of district-level staff development plan to receive Title funding, and school buildings are required to submit similar plans. Organizing your staff training into the categories of literacy, subject-specific, and universal skills is a great way to ensure that your training plan is comprehensive, focused on what matters most, and has something for everyone.

"NO EXCUSES" UNIVERSITIES

All schools, including high-poverty schools, can demonstrate high levels of achievement. We are finally beginning to move beyond excuses. In honor of schools that have found ways around, through, and over obstacles of poverty and language, an organization called Turnaround Schools has begun a movement that is rapidly working its way across the country.

Started by co-principal founders Damen Lopez and Jeff King, Turnaround Schools are committed to creating environments of universal achievement where all students—beginning in kindergarten—are taught to believe they can go to college and are provided with the necessary instruction so that they will have the skills to reach their goal—no excuses. In these "No Excuses" universities, each classroom in the school is "adopted" by a college or university from around the country. Partnerships are formed and commitments are made to help every child be successful. At the time of this writing, there are ten official No Excuses Universities across the country, and interest in the program is growing every day.

To become a No Excuses University, elementary schools must submit an application that includes a video of what their school is doing to create a culture of universal achievement. Once accepted, the network supports and encourages each school toward excellence through two-day institutes and ongoing collaboration. To learn more about the high-quality professional development that is offered through the Turnaround Institutes, visit www.turnaroundschools.com and discover this incredible breakthrough program that is spearheaded not by traveling consultants but by teacher leaders and practicing principals.

INCREASED PROFESSIONAL DEVELOPMENT IN THE BIG FIVE

A wise king once said, "There is nothing new under the sun." The work of Douglas Reeves (2006) has clearly outlined what it takes to create a school where all children can be successful. Starting with his 90-90-90 studies in the 1990s (schools with 90 percent poverty, 90 percent minority population, and 90 percent achievement), and most recently with the discovery of 100-100-100 schools, Reeves has documented five common practices that these high-achieving schools engage in: (1) accountability, (2) nonfiction writing across the curriculum, (3) frequent common assessments, (4) immediate intervention, and (5) constant use of constructive data.

Accountability in these schools moves far beyond annual test scores from the state department. In these high-achieving schools, they impose accountability on every level. Students are accountable for coming to school and learning, parents are accountable for being informed and involved, and teachers are accountable for making sure every child with low skills is receiving the instruction and services he or she needs to be successful. A culture of accountability for learning is present. High expectations are rampant from everyone.

Writing is thinking on paper, and people who think are learners who can solve complex problems. Society needs more from students than memorized math facts. The world of the 21st century needs students who can think and solve problems. Nonfiction writing is the door that opens the mind to complex thinking—in every subject—and schools that actively engage in writing across the curriculum have discovered test score gains in every domain.

Educators realize the value of an aligned common curriculum that clearly defines what students need to learn at each grade level and in every subject. A common curriculum gives teachers markers to help them navigate the vast landscape of knowledge that is growing more and more every day. A common curriculum with identified power standards—not a scripted curriculum—is good for students and prepares them for the future. High-achieving schools take a common curriculum one step further by developing and employing common assessments so that teachers know whether students have actually learned what they were taught. These teachers do not wait for the yearly state test results to tell them how they are doing. They have developed assessments based upon their common curriculum that they can agree on, and they use those assessments to guide instruction.

In the spring, nearly every high school in America plans for failure by creating teaching sections in the master schedule for the numbers of Fs they know students will receive. In most schools, that number ranges from 25 to 40 percent. Most schools haven't been able to figure out a way to prevent the failure they know will occur.

High-achieving schools don't wait for failure. On the contrary, they actively put their energy and resources into immediate interventions. Using frequent formative assessments as a thermometer, they "take the temperature" of their students along the way. Students who fall behind are given extra support, just in time, not after it is too late. In this way, the ugly cycle of acceptable failure is broken, and students begin to realize that no one will allow them to fail.

Those who frequent education circles have been hearing the four-letter word for some time now: data. Data is everywhere, and many are wondering when the fad will fade so we can move on to the next thing. High-performing schools never "get over" data. They use it constantly in constructive ways. They use it to make improvements in the instructional program, to increase attendance, to make the lunchroom a safer place to eat, and to keep the buses running on time. Analyzing data is the pathway to improvement. Teachers who lead also learn to use data in a variety of ways to improve instruction, and data-analyzing principals are key leaders in transforming school environments.

SETTING THE CAPTIVES FREE

In *Prisoners of Time: School and Programs Making Time Work for Students and Teachers* (Jones, 1994), we can begin to understand how valuable and important the resource of time is in our schools. Numbers of hours define our school year. Days of instruction litter our contracts, and the clanging of bells stops and starts instruction in thousands upon thousands of classrooms across the country every day. More than a few high school principals get "new job opportunities" because they dare to alter the sacred schedule of their school. Those who have successfully defied tradition and helped teachers discover new ways to organize and use time are by far the exception rather than the rule.

For many, change does not come easily. We are bound by the universal law that one year of age equals one year of learning, and school systems that have attempted to attach learning to progression through grade levels are consistently branded as outlaws by the statement "Retention doesn't work"—and they are right. If we define retention as doing the same thing over again for another year sentence, it doesn't work, but we also don't have to look any further than the end of the street and talk to a handful of high school teachers to realize that social promotion doesn't work either. Nobody is doing students any favors by delivering them to the doorstep of high school with skills two to three years below grade level.

No matter where you fall on the retention–social promotion continuum, it is still a problem bound by time, and educational leaders are more often than not the wardens of the system defending their biases to left or right with every passing year but rarely pursuing innovations that challenge the status quo.

A few years ago, I saw a picture in the newspaper of a yard surrounded by a fence with buildings in the background. I had to look twice to determine if I was looking at a prison or a school, and it was only by squinting to see the barbed wire winding around the top of the fence that I figured it out. It is no small curiosity to me that the same companies that specialize in school construction also specialize in building prisons.

Empowering teachers to become leaders through effective training and professional development is the first step to break out of the prisons we have created. Principals need to help their teachers see there are other ways of "doing school." Everyone needs a turn in the yard now and then.

Visiting other schools with teams of teachers is a powerful way to discover new ways of organizing time so that it can work for us rather than against us.

Schools can be crazy places, but the most effective school leaders daydream and look forward to the day when the inmates will be running the asylum. At the heart of teacher leadership is the golden hope that teachers will take ownership of the system. Smart principals understand the transforming power of teacher leadership and continually leave the keys lying around, hoping they will get discovered and used to set the captives free.

REFLECT AND RESPOND

Take a moment to dream of the perfect teaching schedule. What would the day look like? How would you be teaching? How would students be learning? If you could have any teaching schedule, what would it be? Can you incorporate any of those concepts into your current assignment? If so, which ones?

TEACHER LEADERSHIP SCENARIO #5: UNPRODUCTIVE STAFF MEETINGS

You are a relatively new principal at a school that is steeped in long-held traditions, and staff meetings at this school are not something to look forward to. Generally they are used for announcements or full-tilt griping. As the principal, you would like to turn things around, but you just aren't sure how to do it. It is starting to annoy you that some teachers bring schoolwork to the meetings. You are responsible for leading the meeting and building the agenda, but teachers will often add things to it that they want to discuss. You are tired of the poor behavior of some staff members, and you feel like the poor climate of the meeting is because of the teachers' bad behavior. What do you do?

Think about what you would do and then turn to appendix A: Teacher Leadership Scenario Responses for a suggestion about how to respond to the scenario listed above.

6

LEADING TO LEARN: CREATING COMMUNITIES OF LEADERS

> I envision a school that is a community of leaders. This is a place whose very mission is to ensure that every student, parent, teacher, and principal will become a school leader in some ways and at some times. . . . It's exciting to speculate about what would happen if, in addition to becoming a community of learners, every school were to become such a community of leaders.
>
> —Roland Barth

Leadership is a constant state of learning. The best leaders are learners, and they are constantly learning in order to build their leadership skills. In my early days as a principal, I spent some time reading Roland Barth's *Learning by Heart* (2001) and was inspired by his vision that leadership in the schoolhouse should be everyone's job.

Using Barth's vision of leadership as a springboard, I designed a full-day workshop called "Leading to Learn." The concept was fairly simple. Learning is the foundation of leading. Therefore, if I as a principal want to lead, I need to be learning. What am I reading? What am I writing? What am I doing to further my own learning? The paradox of the principalship is profound. Most principals are so strapped and stressed moving from one management crisis to the next that they do not have time to learn. However, if they do not have time to learn, they are not qualified to lead effectively. As a result, school improvement efforts are not sustained. Schools will not improve if they are not organizations that continually learn. Leading begins with learning, and the principal must find ways to be the principal learner.

With that foundation in mind, I spent a day with my staff in dialogue about learning and its relationship to leading. We brainstormed what our school would look like if every adult were a leader. What would happen if everyone contributed what he or she had to offer? We realized there would be increased positive interactions, teamwork, cooperation, flexibility, and lots of energy. Everyone would be striving to give his or her best effort. Nothing would be left undone. Needs would be identified and met. We would be good listeners and active responders, willing to do what is necessary for the good of all. There would be open and honest communication. Conflicts would be allowed to surface and be resolved. There would be no hidden agendas.

We realized if every adult were a leader, children would have positive role models. They would see what it looks and sounds like to be responsible. If this occurred, students would take risks to become leaders also. Things that are normally forgotten would be taken care of. We would have a professional environment. Teachers would want to learn by attending conferences, workshops, and classes. They would share their expertise with the rest of the staff in a supportive environment where learning was valued above status, age, and experience.

We also realized there might be some chaos—and that it would be okay. Not everyone would be using the same instructional materials in the same way. People would be trying new strategies they learned about at a conference or from a book. There would be action research projects occurring and an increase of field trip requests and grant applications. The school and staff would get more attention for their success. Success generates more success and improvement. Leading one another would infuse strength in our areas of weakness, and we wouldn't feel bad or inferior for sharing those weaknesses with others. Trust would be paramount. The point was obvious. Becoming a community of leaders would be a wonderful thing for the children of our school, and it would be a wonderful thing for the adults too.

In our daylong workshop, we came to understand that leadership is not a skill set, but a mind-set—that of a learner. By learning, you grow into leadership. We also discussed things that hindered and promoted learning in the classroom. From the intelligence of the group, we discovered the following hindrances to learning:

- Low self-esteem
- A negative environment (physical, mental)
- A lack of support (parental and educational)
- A lack of diversity (which we defined as exposure to experiences and people who are different)
- Inconsistency
- Criticism (negativity in voice inflection and body language)
- Expecting children to learn the same way (a lack of differentiation)
- A lack of opportunity
- Frustration
- External factors
- A lack of role models
- Peer pressure
- Isolation
- Humiliation in front of peers

We also discovered the following elements that supported learning:

- Firsthand experiences (hands-on)
- Encouragement
- Students teaching students
- Support from others
- Variety and differentiation
- A positive environment
- Acknowledging thinking and risk taking
- Recognition of success
- Positive peer pressure
- Continuity and structure
- A community (feeling a part of the whole)
- Clear expectations
- Knowing your students (how they learn and what motivates them)
- Flexibility
- Physical activity
- Healthy lifestyles
- Love (acceptance)
- Respect
- Enjoyable experiences

Clearly defining the elements that both hindered and promoted learning was an outstanding activity that had a direct impact on teachers in the classroom. It gave them opportunities with their peers to discuss not only what they could do to promote learning in their classroom but also what they could do as leaders to remove the barriers to learning.

STAFF ACTIVITY: ENCOURAGING LEARNING

Facilitating a conversation with your staff on what hinders and promotes learning can be a powerful experience. The initial conversation can occur in a 45- to 60-minute time period. Once staff has generated the preliminary list, it can be used to help direct further staff development and school improvement goals. At a staff meeting, write on one side of the board "Things That Hinder Learning." On the other side of the board, write "Things That Support Learning." Have each person reflect and write down at least three elements that hinder and three things that support learning on a piece of paper.

While they are reflecting, have each one think about the best and worst teachers they ever had. What did those teachers do differently? What experiences led to learning and what experiences hindered learning? Next, have the staff members think about times when their own classroom lessons went well and everyone learned. What was special and unique about those lessons? What about lessons that didn't go well— what set those ones apart as poor experiences?

Once everyone has identified at least three things that hinder learning and three that support it, have them share, in groups of two or three, a few of the items on their list along with their good and bad experiences. Sharing in small groups will allow deeper reflection about the experiences.

After 10 to 15 minutes of sharing, have staff members place items on the board they had on their list or shared with others in the room. Begin with the items that hinder learning, and continue around the room listing things until the list is exhaustive. Use the same process to list items that support learning. When you are done, you will have an extensive list of things to avoid in the classroom and a great list of actions to emulate that will support learning. Your lists may look similar to the ones in this book, but your staff will have benefited from the conversation that generated the ideas. Chances are likely each staff member will have identified both a practice he or she wants to start that will support learning and another practice that he or she needs to stop doing.

To make this activity even more beneficial, have each staff member share a lesson that he or she will modify or adjust so that it will be more supportive of learning. You will need more time or another session to do that kind of follow-up work, but it will be well worth the effort.

LEADING INNOVATIONS

When teachers begin innovating, leadership is not far behind. In 1947 a young woman went to college and had a passion for math and science. She wanted to be a geologist, but in those "happy days" there were very few girls in advanced math and science classes in college. As a matter of fact, this young lady was ridiculed by her male teachers and peers and even given "extra" assignments that other students didn't have to do. Eventually, the pressure broke her, and she dropped her course of study. She wound up following the crowd of young ladies into the field of teaching, but she never let go of her passion and worked to incorporate it into her classroom whenever she could.

In 1969, she and another teacher read about a couple of teachers on the East Coast who worked a split contract. They each taught half of the contract days. No one they knew of was doing such a thing on the West Coast, but the idea intrigued these innovators, who both wanted to teach to their strengths and free up time to raise families. They pitched the idea to their superintendent, who gave them an opportunity to innovate with the concept of a "split contract."

The idea turned out to be a smashing success. Not only did the split contract allow the two teachers an opportunity to focus on their passions with a shared group of students, but it also was an innovation for many others. They ended up working together for the next 20 years alternating teaching days, and they watched their idea spread over the years. They were not vocal in their leadership, but they did create a model that many others emulated.

Sharing a class and room required a great deal of coordination and planning. In the 1970s and 1980s, that kind of effort was seen as "extra" work, but it also allowed our teacher leaders an opportunity to pursue their strengths in the field of education and still keep the balance they were seeking in life. Our young geologist was able to focus on math and science while her co-teacher became an expert in reading and social studies. Together, they made a brilliant team, and their students benefited from their innovation.

If we are to create communities of leaders, teachers will need encouragement and opportunities to try new things. One of the ways such encouragement naturally occurs is through the training and development of "Critical Friends Groups."

THE POWER OF CONVERSATION: CRITICAL FRIENDS GROUPS

Critical Friends Groups (CFGs) are becoming more and more important for educators across the country. Teachers and administrators alike are being trained as CFG coaches to facilitate high-quality conversations between teachers where real-world problem solving and capacity building can occur. According to the National School Reform Faculty (NSRF, 2007), CFGs are a professional learning community consisting of 8–12 educators who come together voluntarily at least once a month.

The Annenberg Institute for School Reform at Brown University first developed the Critical Friends model in the mid-1990s. Since that time, the movement has been picked up by several organizations, including the Coalition for Essential Schools and the National School Reform Faculty Program. Critical, in the context of the group, is intended to be positive—meaning "important," "key," or "necessary," as opposed to a negative connotation. One of the chief goals of the movement is to provide a structure for facilitating honest, meaningful dialogue between colleagues that will have a direct impact upon classroom instruction, learning, and student achievement.

In July 2000, the National School Reform Faculty Program, which currently houses Critical Friends Groups and coordinates training across the country for Critical Friends Coaches, moved to the Harmony School

Education Center (HSEC) in Bloomington, Indiana. Detailed information about the movement, including training opportunities, can be found on their website at www.nsrfharmony.org and at www.cesnorthwest.org.

CFG meetings are organized and structured by a facilitator, who sets time limits and manages the process of the meeting to ensure that specific protocols are followed. Facilitators are trained coaches who have learned a variety of strategies to help make the meetings productive for everyone. In addition to a facilitator, the group also contains presenters and discussants. As originally developed, there are three types of Critical Friends protocols: (1) peer observations, (2) tuning a teaching artifact using the Tuning Process, and (3) consulting about an issue using the Consultancy Process. Over the course of time, several other CFG protocols have been developed, including Collaborative Assessment, Chalk Talk, Descriptive Review, Text-Based Seminar, and Final Word, just to name a few. To help understand how CFGs operate in a school, I've included a couple protocol examples in the following text.

CFG: *Consultancy Process*

In the Consultancy Process, anyone in the group can be a presenter. The presenter brings an issue for "consultancy" and is clear about the question or problems she is bringing. The presenter can bring forward an issue that is bothering her, student work she would like analyzed, questions about something she read, or a host of other real-world problems she is encountering as a teacher. After presenting the issue, the discussants have an opportunity to ask clarifying questions about the dilemma in order to understand it fully.

Once the problem has been clarified, the discussants have 15 minutes to discuss the problem and try to generate some answers. The presenter does not participate during this time but instead simply takes notes on what is discussed, being sure to record anything helpful. After the discussion, the presenter has an opportunity to respond to the group feedback. The session concludes with the facilitator debriefing what occurred.

Since it takes about 45 minutes to process an issue using this protocol, a CFG can deal in depth with two issues that are brought forward during a 90-minute session. In addition to the presenter receiving warm (supportive) and cool (key or critical) feedback to her issue, the others in the group also benefit from the conversation. Critical Friends Groups support teacher leadership because they function completely without hierarchy. Teachers and administrators participate voluntarily and exchange roles depending on their training. CFGs must be built on mutual respect and trust to be effective. If they are not, the participants will not bring forward serious or complex issues for processing.

CFG: Tuning Protocol

The "Tuning" Protocol is a formalized way to get feedback on work in progress or to examine student work. To use this protocol, the facilitator begins by introducing the goals, guidelines, and time schedule. A member of the CFG (the "Tunee") brings forward a work in progress, student artifact, or other document he would like some feedback on. The rest of the group serves as "Tuners" and listens to the Tunee's explanation of the piece. After the initial presentation, the Tuners can ask clarifying questions about the work. The Tunee can also ask for specific feedback during this time: warm, cool, or hard. Warm feedback is positive points associated with the work. Cool feedback would be considered questions that arise, doubts, or gaps in the work. Hard feedback refers to challenges related to the work.

Similar to the Consultancy Process, the Tunee does not participate during the discussion but instead listens and takes notes. After the feedback session, the Tunee has an opportunity to reflect upon what was discussed, and the session concludes with the facilitator debriefing what occurred.

Descriptions of the CFG process may be helpful, but the best advocates for CFGs are teacher leaders who have participated in the process.

My school has participated in the CFG training, and we are just starting to use those protocols and processes. I participated in a Critical Friends Group and I think the major part of it is the way people respond to each other. All people in the group are given a chance to speak and others must listen without interruption or response. At first I found it frustrating because of all of the wait time, but it does give the person talking some freedom to express without interruption or fear of what someone will say once they are done. Also, if a person comes to the group with a problem, there is a procedure of how to help. Rather than just throwing out all the different opinions to help the teacher, the procedure allows the teacher to respond and explain more as well as take notes on the solutions. There are a lot of rules but it forces others to participate and act respectfully. It is something we always ask of our students, but don't practice ourselves. (Elementary Teacher)

RESOLVING CONFLICT

Resolving conflict is one of the chief roles of leaders. Whether the conflict begins on the playground, in the cafeteria, or in the classroom down the hall, schools are full of conflicts, and most of them wind up in the principal's office. Good principals are problem solvers and negotiators—they have to be in order to survive. When students, parents, or staff experience conflict that cannot get resolved, it usually flows to the principal's office. However, there is grave danger in a principal stepping in too often or always having to be the one with the "final word."

Principals who develop and support teacher leaders have learned the art of building the capacity of those around them by sharing leadership. Whenever possible, they create opportunities for others to get involved. In this way, the community learns that solutions do not always come from the office.

One smart principal I worked with wanted to investigate different scheduling options for her middle school. Instead of trying to come up with a plan on her own, she got a team of teachers interested in the topic and let them run with it. They did research across the state on different schedules that middle schools were using. They looked at demographic data and test scores. After some time, they brought in data to compare the schools, and it was only after the list was narrowed down to schools they wanted to visit that the principal was brought into the conversation.

Many school leaders would be threatened by this apparent lack of control from the principal's office, but such is not the case for principals who are working hard to share the load and develop teacher leaders. Teacher leaders flatten an organization. They provide increased hubs in the network so that more work gets done because more people are helping out. When leadership is distributed, problem solving is distributed as well, and as a result, principals can spend more of their time as instructional leaders and less of their time resolving conflicts.

Conflict will occur in any system because systems are comprised of people. Most people do not like conflict and as a result have a natural tendency to avoid it or pretend it does not exist. Unfortunately, this strategy will only make matters worse because unresolved conflict grows, spreads, and does damage to the system. Effective leaders recognize this tendency and share the power to resolve problems.

REFLECT AND RESPOND

How does your school support the concept of leadership for all? What are some ways you can help your school expand the leadership capacity of all staff, students, and parents?

TEACHER LEADERSHIP SCENARIO #6:
LEAVING THE PACK

As a teacher, you have several leadership roles at your school, and you enjoy being involved and helping make the school better. However, you hear through the grapevine that some teachers don't appreciate your willingness to lead all the time and think you are a "prima donna." How do you respond? In the midst of this dilemma, the district office asks you to lead a seminar on a new instructional strategy you and some others have been using in your building. Do you take on this new project knowing you are already stretched thin and the project may further alienate you from your peers? What do you do?

Think about what you would do and then turn to appendix A: Teacher Leadership Scenario Responses for a suggestion about how to respond to the scenario listed above.

7

SUPPORTING TEACHER LEADERSHIP THROUGH INNOVATION AND REFLECTION

> I really don't know how I get them all reading. I just
> believe they can and don't stop teaching until they do.
>
> —Special Education Teacher

R isk taking does not occur in education circles very often. Public schools are supported by public money, and unlike the for-profit world, our existence does not depend upon our ability to innovate, change, and improve. Recent legislation, such as the federal No Child Left Behind Act, has attempted to change schools through a variety of sanctions if test scores don't improve in math and reading. At first glance, the intentions of NCLB were noble enough to garner bipartisan support, but with the myopic focus on reading and math tests the barons of accountability are beginning to leave bruises on the very schools and children they are trying to serve.

Across the nation, test scores are improving slightly over time but are children more prepared to be successful beyond their K–12 education experience? Are more children graduating from high school and going to college? Are they more prepared to achieve in college? Do they finish college? Do they have the necessary skills to be successful in the workplace? Are more students qualified to pursue careers in the skilled trades? These are the questions we need to be asking at the local, state, and federal levels.

National surveys reveal school boards and the public care more about educating the whole child than improving math and reading test scores (Rothstein & Jacobsen, 2007). There is renewed interest and concern about the eating and exercise habits of children, their ability to use technology to solve complex problems, decision-making skills, character education, appreciation and expression of art, and career awareness planning.

The time, energy, and resources deployed to make sure everyone is tested and improving on those tests is in direct competition with these other priorities, and states are beginning to resent the federal intrusion of requirements without the promised increase of resources to meet the higher demands (American Association of School Administrators, 2007). Local school districts are struggling with the increased requirements as well, but there are some who are striving to meet the needs of their local community in spite of the increased pressure to conform to federal mandates.

SPRINGFIELD'S QUALITY EDUCATION MODEL (S-QEM)

In the fall of 2003, Springfield Public Schools in Oregon launched a yearlong process to find out what the community valued in a public education. Eight attributes surfaced as critical and necessary components for a well-rounded K–12 education. Those attributes are: academic competency, life skills, self-management, cultural competency, character competency, social competency, educational opportunities, and career skills. The eight attributes can be organized into four big ideas and are depicted in figure 7.1: Academics, Relating to Self, Relating to Others, and Future Forward.

Most likely, the results don't surprise you. We all want our children to have more than academic skills. We want them to be able to manage their time properly, know how to treat others with decency, and plan for their future. Just about any community in America will choose similar attributes when surveyed. However, what the school board and district leaders choose to do with that information is what sets them apart as an innovative school system. Springfield Public Schools immediately set aside funding to support schools and teachers to implement the vision and values of the S-QEM.

TEACHER LEADERS NEED RESOURCES

Out of Springfield's $75 million general fund budget, $100,000 may not seem like very much, but it was a start and more than was ever available

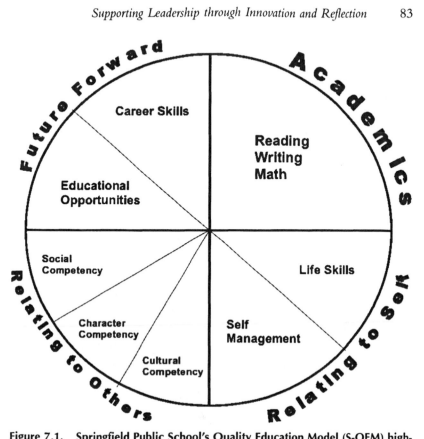

Figure 7.1. Springfield Public School's Quality Education Model (S-QEM) highlights the importance of developing the whole child through today's K–12 education system.

before. After three years of implementation, the investment is making a difference. More than 80 S-QEM projects have been supported throughout the district during the past three years, and each one targets one or more of the attributes of the S-QEM. Most of them are innovative projects brought forward by a teacher or team of teachers who are developing leadership skills by taking on the project.

At one of the high schools, a special education teacher wanted her students to gain firsthand knowledge about skilled careers. She received S-QEM funds to help host a regional conference at the local community college. The conference not only featured representatives from state and local organizations to share information about job opportunities, but it also had breakout sessions so that students could learn about different careers and the requirements necessary to enter those careers.

In addition, there were several demonstration stations where students learned about careers in the trades. The event was much more than the traditional career fair in the gym where students wander through with stamp cards collecting trinkets and gum. It was truly a learning experience about future options and the importance of making plans to pursue meaningful careers.

Many educators, students, and parents don't realize the tremendous opportunity that currently exists for students to follow careers and earn living wages via the skilled trades. National studies are telling us out of every 100 freshmen entering high school, only 15 of them will receive a college degree four to six years after their high school graduation (Graves & Wood, 2006). For the remaining 85 percent, learning and understanding about skilled trades can be a life-changing experience that will provide them with postsecondary options far beyond the local low-paying customer service job.

Another high school teacher leader wanted to increase excitement and knowledge about science at the middle school level, so he organized a Science Olympics for students from across the district and hosted it at his school. Hundreds of sixth- through eighth-graders converged on the high school campus and participated in a variety of hands-on science activities and events. Lunch and T-shirts were provided as well as recognition and medals.

It was an outstanding event that not only emphasized the fact that science can be fun but was also a first step in helping make the difficult transition between middle school and high school a little smoother. The event would not have happened without a supportive high school principal willing to "interrupt" learning at his school with an infusion of middle school students on his campus. This smart principal saw the bigger picture that creating transition activities between levels may be time intensive in the short run but in the long run will pay dividends in student achievement, success, and community support.

Another teacher combined her passion for service learning and art by creating a project called Art-in-Motion. Her project entailed taking high school students trained in videography and art to elementary schools and working with teachers to provide art-based experiences for the students. This project was win-win-win, because not only did the elementary students receive art instruction they couldn't get from their own teacher, but the elementary teachers learned new skills as well. The high school students grew through the experience, and the teacher who sponsored the project developed her leadership skills.

These are just a few of the many projects that have been supported by S-QEM funding. There are also projects where teachers have acquired new technology and measured the impact these programs had on teaching and learning. Staff has received funds to attend trainings to implement new reading and writing programs, schoolwide reading motivation projects, curriculum alignment software and training, proficiency-based credit projects, art integration, and a host of other innovative projects and activities.

At the heart of each project is a passionate teacher, dreaming and thinking about ways to improve education in the classroom so that students will be more engaged and better prepared to face their future. In every case, teacher leadership is strengthened and supported through the innovative grant-funding structure.

THE POWER AND PROMISE OF REFLECTION

There are a couple things that my reflective practices have taught me this year. (1) You can learn important information about kids, families, and teaching from conversations with other people. (2) Reflecting may help you to understand or interpret something different than you might have initially. (3) It helps you to think back over what was done and how things can be made better the next time. (Elementary Teacher)

The discipline of reflection is one of the most powerful tools for developing teacher leaders. Reflection about teaching and learning can occur in three different ways: thinking, writing, and conversations. Reflection through thinking happens when teachers think about their practice, read books or articles about teaching and learning, or consider lessons or units they have taught or will teach. Some of the most effective reflective thinking occurs when teachers are doing activities unrelated to work, like exercising, doing the dishes, or driving. Notice how this teacher leader thinks about her day:

> The one thing that I do really well is not reflecting, but perhaps "pre-flecting." I always find a few minutes of quiet time every morning in my classroom and think about the possible challenges that the day could bring. I visualize how I am going to talk to students and I even pick out a few kids in my head who need some extra attention and pray for them. On days that I do this, I find that I rarely lose my patience, and have a better day altogether. (Middle School Science Teacher)

Writing or journaling is a powerful way to work through thoughts and ideas about teaching and learning. There are many different types of journaling, but the key is not making writing a chore. Don't put any rules on your journaling. If you don't feel like writing anything for six months, then don't. Out of the blue you may get a spurt of ideas and fill up a dozen pages in a couple of days. There are two types of writing when it comes to reflection: the generation of ideas and putting those ideas in a form that others can understand.

Journaling is a great way to generate ideas. Journals are places to jot down or sketch out ideas, questions, or problems. The generation of ideas is not linear. They happen—or don't happen—randomly. Getting those ideas in a form that others can learn from, however, is disciplined work. You have to set time limits, show up, and get busy.

It is important to celebrate small accomplishments in your writing. The more you write, the more confidence you will develop as a writer. Being committed to writing on a regular basis will make you a more effective teacher. That is why having to take classes for advanced degrees and being forced to write is a good thing—even though it is not always easy. The research connecting writing to an increased ability to think and problem solve is well established, but you have to find a system that works for you.

The third method of reflection is through conversation and dialogue with others. Learning does not happen in isolation. We need each other. The power of Critical Friends Groups (CFGs) is built on conversations. Dialogue can be formalized and organized through learning teams or grade-level teams, but informal conversations about teaching and learning through book studies can be a powerful method of reflection as well.

> Reflecting with my mentor teacher has been invaluable to my teaching. While I reflect with her, we are able to brainstorm solutions to problems and encourage each other in best practices. I have the benefit of learning from the craft knowledge she has acquired over the last 20 years. During our reflection time, she often has insight into students that we share or she has previously taught. This insight helps me better address the needs of the students. After our discussions, I feel better prepared to function with other colleagues at my school and with my students inside my classroom. (Elementary Teacher)

I recently heard of a principal who had his staff write on a regular basis in meetings, and share that writing with other staff members. Though it sounds odd at first, this turned out to be an extremely effective way to improve instruction through teacher expertise and build confidence in writing at the same time. All of the teachers became better writers, and as a result, they were able to teach their children to become writers as well.

STAFF ACTIVITY: WHAT IF?

This activity combines the importance of reflection connected to innovation. It can be used to help teachers think about ways teaching and learning can be improved in their classroom and share those ideas with others. Through the sharing process, principals will learn more about what their teachers value and can try to discover ways to support those values so that teacher leadership is developed. This activity will work best in a group of 15 to 30 people but can be accommodated for larger staff meetings.

Begin the meeting by defining reflection and stating its importance to learning. You can use some of the quotes listed in this book or come up with some of your own. Stress that there are many ways to reflect about teaching: thinking about what you taught or will teach, discussing your teaching with others formally or informally, and writing or journaling your ideas about teaching and student learning.

Do the following in order to get an idea of how your staff prefers to reflect. After sharing your definition give each person ten "units of reflection" and ask them to place those units on a sheet of paper in one of three columns: Thinking, Discussing, or Writing according to how they currently reflect about their practice. Remind them that everyone reflects about their practice in some form or fashion, and they must place all ten units in the columns. For example, activities like reading educational books would fall under the category of Thinking. Developing lesson plans would generally fall under the category of Writing unless they are collaborating on those plans with others or simply thinking about what they will do.

In addition to the placement of the units, have them estimate the amount of time they currently spend in reflection about teaching and learning. Remind them that time spent thinking while driving, working in the garden, or decompressing through dialogue with friends counts as well, and that you are only asking for a rough weekly estimate of time.

After they have made their decisions, have them share with a few other people in the room where they placed their units and their reasoning behind their choices. Then on the other side of the paper, have them place the units in the columns according to how they would like to spend their time reflecting in the future. Some of the staff will want to shift their energy and priorities based upon the conversations they've had. Have them also record the amount of time per week they would like to reflect on teaching and learning. After they make their choices, use a four-corners activity so that staff can meet others who have similar goals.

Begin the four-corners activity by placing signs in the four corners of the room according to the following choices: Thinking, Discussing, Writing, Balance. Staff who want to spend the majority of their reflection time thinking will go to one corner. Those who want to do discussion to another, writing to the third, and finally staff members who want to pursue a truly balanced approach will move to the final corner.

Once in their respective corners, have staff members share with one another why they chose that corner. This is a forced-choice activity so it will generate discussion. Conclude this activity by having each group reflect upon the following topic according to their corner of choice: Without increasing resources, what is one innovative strategy or project I can do in my classroom? This prompt should be on the bottom of the piece of paper they have been using to record how they want to spend their units. Each corner group will approach the prompt a little differently. The Writing corner may jot down ideas to share. The Thinking crowd might all go for a walk or draw a picture—that's OK. The Discussion group will begin talking, and the Balanced group will do some of each depending on their preference.

After 15 to 20 minutes of this activity, convene the entire staff in one large group and have volunteers share their response to the prompt. This activity will be beneficial on many levels. Staff will see the value of reflection, hopefully make some decisions about intentionally spending more time to reflect in the future, and share with the rest of the staff resource-free ideas they have for improving teaching and learning in their classrooms.

CONNECT THE DOTS:
THE POWER AND PROMISE OF BELIEF

Every school system has teachers who are doing extraordinary instruction with children. The key to school and district improvement is discovering those islands of excellence and helping other teachers and principals learn about what is happening in the field so they can generate ideas to improve their own classroom and school. I call it connecting the dots. By connecting enough dots over time, a systemic image of excellence will emerge.

I once met a woman who could "teach rocks to read." She was a special education teacher with a self-contained classroom of elementary school children. The children in her room were all labeled severely mentally retarded. Many of them had IQs in the 40s, and the disabilities in her room ranged from cerebral palsy to severe autism. In this K–5 classroom, each child came from a school around the district with a sad story, and most of the sad stories had one common theme: This child can't learn. Each child came to her classroom to be housed, and few expected little else to occur. However, to this indomitable teacher, the greater the challenge, the more determined she became.

Success after success with the "unteachable" children built her reputation over time as one of the best. One child came to her room in a

manual wheelchair with cerebral palsy. He was nonverbal but could vo-
calize sounds. He was said to be so distractible that he couldn't eat lunch
with others and would need a one-to-one assistant at all times to try and
keep him on task. After some time in her classroom, the boy began to
show huge gains. He stopped being distracted. He started reading and independently typing. He learned how to use a motorized wheelchair and
didn't need constant attention from an adult to prevent distraction. It
turned out his distraction was not connected to his disability at all. Deep
down, it was a choice. His teacher believed the student had a choice all
along, and it was precisely this belief that created the opportunity for
him to become a learner.

On another occasion, a nearly nonverbal kindergartener with a reported IQ of 42, who would giggle if asked to do anything and was un-
able to focus, track, or pay attention in any way, arrived and couldn't remember letter names and sounds. Two weeks in "the room" and this
child had learned letter names and sounds and was reading pre-primer
materials. District personnel observing success after success wondered
how this teacher could accomplish so much in a crowded classroom (she
had 20 of these high-needs students assigned to her class) without core
curriculum. Is it really such a mystery?

How did Annie Sullivan make a learner out of Helen Keller without core curriculum? The federal government recently published a report stating they couldn't find consistent student achievement increases
through the use of expensive educational technology materials and
methods (National Council on Economic Education, 2007). Should we
really be surprised? Haven't we learned by now that learning is a prod-
uct of the teacher, not the materials the teacher is using? Highly trained,
effective teachers trump every other factor, including poverty, designa-
tion as an English-language learner, placement in special education, instructional materials, and now even technology. When it comes to teaching, the bottom line is still the most important one of all: Effective
teachers believe all children can learn, and they are relentless in finding
ways to help all of their children succeed. They do not make excuses—
any excuses.

They do not make excuses about class size, disability, poverty, par-
enting, workload, the weather, or materials. On the contrary, they take
pleasure in overcoming odds. Their mantra is a simple one, "Get out of

the way and let me teach!" Without exception—across all professions— such an attitude is the trademark of all great leaders, and great leadership will manifest itself in outstanding results every time.

REFLECT AND RESPOND

What is your belief system about teaching and learning? How do you demonstrate the belief that all children can learn and achieve? Do you ever catch yourself drifting into "unbelief" in this area? Why? How do you sustain the belief that all children can learn? Do you have any stories of "unteachable" children who beat the odds?

TEACHER LEADER SCENARIO #7: NEW KID ON THE BLOCK

You are a new teacher in an old building, and it is old in more ways than one. The most debilitating elements about your new assignment are the current staff members. They have made it clear in more ways than one that your voice is not valued. You haven't figured out the principal yet, but you feel there won't be a whole lot of support from that office either. You really want to make a difference but are constantly on edge about what is acceptable and not acceptable. It seems that the staff's main mission is to make excuses and defend the status quo, and you want to make improvements. What do you do?

Think about what you would do and then turn to appendix A: Teacher Leadership Scenario Responses for a suggestion about how to respond to the scenario listed above.

8

BALANCING TEACHER
LEADERSHIP

My philosophy has become, the day after the kids go home
for the summer and my grades are submitted, I am caught
up. Other than that, I am never caught up so what is one
more thing?

—Middle School Teacher

Teaching is a stressful and demanding profession. For the greater portion of every day, teachers work in isolation with dozens of children
of varying abilities, maturity, likes, dislikes, family backgrounds, culture
backgrounds, social status, and personality types. Teachers make thousands of decisions every hour in order to meet the learning, emotional,
and physical needs of the children in their care. How is it possible for
teachers to handle the daily stress of teaching, have lives outside of school,
and step into leadership roles? There is a one-word answer: balance.

Balance is the key. There will always be more needs than we can
possibly meet. The trick is learning how to choose the projects and activities that will have the most impact and putting your energy toward
those activities. Celebrate small successes and don't be overwhelmed by
what isn't getting done. Focus on what is happening rather than what is
not. Being a leader for the long haul also means knowing when to walk
away and leave your schoolwork behind.

Strongly supporting family will pay future dividends. Some schools
develop unspoken cultures where people are inwardly competing to see
who can arrive the earliest or stay the latest to show their "dedication"
and "commitment" to the school. They want others to notice how much
time they are working and drop little phrases about coming in on the
weekend, staying until 7 P.M., or arriving at 6 A.M.

As a principal, I never encouraged or supported that kind of behavior. Putting in more hours doesn't make you a more effective teacher. It is how you use your time, not how time much you use. It's important not to look down at a teacher who doesn't stay late or come early. Teachers *should* have lives outside of school. It makes them well-rounded human beings, prevents burnout, and promotes balance.

Teacher burnout is a big issue, and one of the best ways to combat it is through teacher leadership—sharing the load. As more people take on leadership roles, the work doesn't become overwhelming for just a few people. It is the administration's responsibility to do whatever possible to get more people involved and encourage all staff to take on some leadership roles. It is not healthy for the individual teacher, school, or system to have the same people serving on all the committees and going to all of the conferences and workshops. Once a principal finds a few willing souls, it is a big temptation to keep shouldering them with reform efforts, but in the long run it is a mistake. More work will get done and burnout will be avoided when everyone gets involved.

STAFF ACTIVITY: THE REWARDS OF INVOLVEMENT

What rewards make teacher leadership worth the effort? For me, it is relationships and making a difference. Whether it is coaching volleyball and getting to know students in a different light or collaborating with a group of teachers reviewing new textbooks—the process of building relationships with these individuals makes all the extra time invested in these activities worth it. The involvement in a leadership role that makes a difference for a student, teacher, group of individuals, the school, or community is also very satisfying. (Middle School Teacher)

Leadership is its own reward. The goal of this activity is to help teachers see the value of stepping into leadership roles. On a piece of paper, have your staff reflect via writing for ten minutes on the following topics:

1. What is leadership?
2. Name someone who had a leadership influence in your life.
3. What influence did they have and how did it help you?

After they have written down some thoughts, have them share those thoughts in groups of three people. Give staff at least 15 minutes to share and then instruct the groups to discuss a time when they personally stepped into a leadership role and share the value or benefit of that role. After another five to ten minutes of sharing, encourage volunteers from each small group to share with the whole group the benefits their members experienced by participating in leadership roles. Conclude the session by asking what kinds of current leadership roles are available at the school and what kinds of roles could be made available.

Providing opportunities for staff members to interact with each other is the best use of staff time. This activity will encourage reflection through writing and dialogue. It can be completed in a 45-minute time period with a staff of any size. It will help teachers to remember not only how their lives were improved by the leadership of others but also times when they were able to be leaders. Concluding the session by having staff reflect on ways to demonstrate leadership at the school will allow their passions to surface. Leadership is hard work, and everyone is working hard already. It is important to let staff follow their passions when it comes to leadership. No one is interested in sitting on another meaningless committee, but they are interested in making a difference. Provide those kinds of opportunities whenever possible.

INERTIA: UNSUPPORTIVE ADMINISTRATORS

One of the biggest barriers to teacher leadership is poor management. That is why the Dilbert comic strip is so funny, and *The Office* TV show is so compelling. We laugh because we can relate. Stupidity is entertaining—unless you are in the middle of it. Schools are places of tradition, and there are many traditions that no longer make sense but we continue to do them because they have become a part of the system.

The bell schedule is just one example. Think of everything in schools that is tied to the almighty ringing of the bells. Whether it is every 45 minutes, 60 minutes, or 90 minutes, the clanging of the bells defines the instructional day and prevents doing anything different than teaching in those defined blocks of time. When schools begin to design their instructional program around student needs, they start becoming flexible with blocks of time and eventually kill the bells. Once dead, they generally do not return. Most schools will keep them silent, and strangely enough students are still able to get to class on time. Everyone grows calmer, and the teacher is recognized as the one who starts and stops instruction.

It takes supportive administrators to alter the status quo through teacher leadership. When administrators are not supportive, the system generally remains intact regardless of how much effort teachers put into changing it—that is the law of leadership, and the reason why quality leadership is so crucial in schools today. The system will never be able to rise above the quality of its leader. Hopefully, there have been enough examples throughout this book of ways administrators can support teacher leadership in their schools, because no matter how many great ideas come from teachers, management can easily get in the way of those ideas by not providing the necessary support or resources. Improvement requires change, and change involves risk—on everyone's part.

LEARN TO TAKE RISKS

I think I have taken a lot of risks in the past few years. Most of these risks were simply saying yes to opportunities presented to me. Many times, after saying yes, I panicked a little about what I had gotten myself into. Some of these things failed miserably and others have been a wonderful part of my development as a professional. One huge risk I took was saying yes to piloting a technology program in my classroom having little experience with technology myself. I have grown so much as an educator because of this program and it has led me on other paths as well. The staff at my school make it pretty easy to take risks and try new things. I have come to realize that a supporting staff and good friends are essential for teachers to take risks. (Middle School Teacher)

We have already touched on the connection of risk taking to teacher leadership, but what are the components within a school that support risk taking? When people feel supported, they are able to take risks, and when teachers step into new leadership roles, they will need support from their peers and supervisors. Risk taking can be learned behavior, but it won't be practiced if people get in trouble every time a risk is taken.

A teacher once told me, "Anything worth doing is worth doing badly at first." I am in complete agreement with that statement. That is one of the chief reasons I would much rather spend my time implementing a vision as opposed to writing a plan. Get out there and fail at something. Make some noise. Don't let people with negative fantasies slow you down. School improvement is not for the faint of heart. It is exhausting work. There are no cookie-cutter solutions, no quick fixes, no "out of the box" recipes. There are only key components, and teacher leadership is right at the top of the list. However, teacher leadership does not emerge without teachers willing to take risks, and teachers will rarely take risks if they are not constantly supported and encouraged in their risk taking.

A middle school was divided into grade-level teams and each team had four staff members who shared cohorts of students. Though the theory of grade-level teams is worthy, unfortunately schools are not staffed according to their vision. They are staffed according to students who walk through the door, and in this particular school, the numbers didn't match the staff. As a result, there was one teacher left over who wasn't part of a team. With the support of administration, this teacher adapted her interests to the need at hand and created an all-day natural resources focus class.

Students were placed in this all-day program according to their interest and over the course of several years a variety of integrated projects developed from the structure. The students engaged in service learning throughout the neighborhood and even adopted a local park that the city didn't have the resources to maintain. The self-contained class made the natural resources curriculum possible, and the students excelled in this unique program. The successful implementation only occurred because one teacher was willing to take a series of risks, and she was encouraged by supportive administration. Like most successful ventures, it was a team effort.

There are some who would argue that age is the determining factor in someone's willingness to take risks. However, learning is more closely connected to risk taking than age. Through learning, we can overcome our fears, and without fear, we are more willing to try new things. I do not support the stereotype that often surfaces between "old" and "young" teachers because I have seen too many "old" teachers acting like "new" ones and vice versa.

Age is time bound, but youth is not bound by time. The "young" are open to new ideas, and the "old" have made up their minds. I have met "old" young teachers freshly minted from teacher preparation programs with all the answers—not willing to learn. I have also had the privilege to work with and know many "young" old teachers who were constantly learning new strategies, investing in professional development, and taking on new assignments and roles in schools year after year.

There are stages in life and teachers shouldn't be expected to be everything for everyone all the time. Sometimes it's good to be "old" (stubborn—especially when it comes to high expectations for students), and most of the time it is good to be "young" (flexible—especially when it comes to thriving in a changing world). There are advantages to all stages of life. If we are fortunate, we will get an opportunity to live in each stage. We should enjoy the benefits of each one. How many young people do you know who want to be old? And how many old people do you know who want to be young? Happy are those who are content in their stage. Learning is the fountain of youth. Learning transcends age, and those who learn are constantly renewing themselves.

DETERMINING PRIORITIES

Teacher leaders have the opportunity to create a positive school culture, bring about change, and influence others. We will be constantly asked to add more to our plates. We need to say no to some duties, but remember to say yes to the ideas that will make our careers more meaningful. (High School Social Studies Teacher)

In schools where leadership is distributed, no one person is carrying too much of the load. The burden of service that leaders must bear is shared by many, and the blessings associated with serving are shared as well. When leadership is shared, more work gets done.

There are two kinds of people: those who get things done and those who don't. The first group is composed of action-oriented people and the second group likes to talk—and usually when they are talking, they are complaining. You can generally determine what kind of person someone is by how much time he or she spends complaining. High complainers are generally not people of action.

Teacher leaders are people of action, but the action-oriented always run the risk of trying to do too much. Surrounded by needs, they are constantly taking on new projects and activities. As a result, they run the risk of spreading themselves too thin and not able to bring things home and finish the job. Learning how to determine what your priorities are and how to stick to those priorities is critical for people of action. Ongoing reflection (via dialogue, writing, or thinking) is the best way to ferret out low-yield activities so that your energy can be funneled into projects that will generate the greatest results for your efforts. The discipline of asking questions is a great way to practice ongoing reflection. Some of the key questions for teacher leaders are:

1. What am I learning?
2. How am I meeting student needs?
3. How am I being supportive of my colleagues?
4. What am I currently doing that is of little value to my work?
5. If I stopped doing a particular activity, would anyone notice?

Creating a "stop doing list" is a great technique to help action-oriented leaders get more done, and questions 4 and 5 are the starting point for creating such a list. Are you spending too much time responding to e-mail? Are you creating paragraphs when simple sentences will work? E-mail is a great tool for simple communication, but it is no substitute for real conversations with people, and using it to replace face-to-face or voice-to-voice contact can be a huge time drain. Too much time on e-mail is just one thing that might end up on your "stop doing list." Add in TV watching, Internet surfing, and newspaper/magazine reading, and you are on your way to redeeming valuable time.

RESISTERS

Unfortunately, I can't help think that there are so many times when teachers are trying to take on leadership roles but face tremendous opposition. Other teachers are feeling threatened by anyone who may "outdo" them or promote a change that they are not comfortable with. Many of the teacher leaders I interviewed said they thought the other staff members were untrusting of them and suspicious. This type of attitude is truly tragic. Because there is such opposition to change, these untrusting teachers are actually perpetuating an unhealthy culture in their school. It seems ironic that the very thing that may be holding education back are other educators. It is a situation that is disheartening to say the least. (Elementary Teacher)

Teacher leaders will face resistance, and that resistance will come from a variety of sources: peers, supervisors, and lack of resources, just to name a few. Learning how to work around and through external obstacles that prevent teacher leadership is critical. The most successful teacher leaders I've known overcome these external resisters through determination and by focusing on the end result—improving education and quality of life for their students.

Every day, fresh ideas just trying to sprout their wings get shot down because someone on staff makes the comment, "We tried that already. It won't work." Energetic teachers who want to start an after-school club may face a colleague telling them not to do it because it would put pressure on the rest of the staff to do something. Not having enough resources has stalled many a project, but determined teacher leaders have a knack for working through these difficulties and many more. Nothing worthwhile is easy. Making a difference will always be a struggle, but in the end, the benefits outweigh the difficulties.

Internal resisters to teacher leadership are generally more difficult to deal with because they are personal in nature and usually involve self and family. Most teachers have families of their own, and dedicating massive amounts of energy and resources into a classroom can leave a mark on family life. Balance is the key for dealing with internal resisters.

If you are in this business for the long haul, it is important to know where the boundaries are on the home front and stay within the markers. Taking time to exercise, eat right, play, and get rest when needed are also important to balancing your own personal needs. Though spectators may get excited about fast starts, it is only those who finish the race who get the prize. Approaching internal resisters with balance is a surefire way you can ensure a successful run across the finish line.

I spent part of today with an amazing teacher who discussed teacher leadership and didn't bring up any of the above resisters. She spoke with passion for her job, love of her students, and appreciation of education. She was completely positive about the teaching profession. When asked what importance teacher leadership has she stated, "Essential." I looked up essential in the dictionary and it was defined as "fundamental, necessary and indispensable." I agree. (High School Teacher)

THE PROCESS OF CHANGE IN SCHOOLS

Change is rocky business—especially in education. Educational reform has been around for some time, but despite a whole lot of resources, effort, and energy, we haven't moved very far. Most of the time it seems like schools and districts are spinning their wheels and not getting much traction for their efforts. We think we are moving because the scenery is changing and there is a lot of activity happening, but we might just be going in big circles. The wheels on the bus are not moving together in the same direction, and we regift the same old reforms in new packages with new price tags. Teacher leadership, on the other hand, is an effective catalyst for improvement and meaningful change in a positive direction because it is organic and grows within a school rather than being brought in from the outside.

There are two types of organizations: nonprofit (the social sector) and profit (the business sector). It is easier to be successful in the business sector as an agent of change because business leaders have more authoritative power. They tell people to change, and if they don't, they find someone else who will. In the world of nonprofits, leaders have a great deal of legislative power and not as much authoritative power. They have to convince people to change.

Teacher leaders—especially new ones—are in an even more precarious place than principals. They do not have legislative or authoritative power. Can you hear the chorus, "Who do you think you are telling me how to teach! You've only been teaching for a few years." Teachers can be proud, self-reliant, and downright stubborn when it comes to their craft. The system has trained them to be that way to survive. Whatever authoritative power exists in a school belongs to the principal, and for this reason, principals are key players when it comes to unleashing and supporting teacher leadership throughout the school.

THE COMFORT OF THE STATUS QUO

Change is difficult because it is unknown. We are all comfortable with the familiar, even if what we are doing is less successful. Throughout my career, I've been able to institute a great deal of change without replacing staff. Perhaps I've been lucky, but if you are supportive, then people will be willing to try new things, and when the new things work, they will not only keep doing them but will work hard to defend them, and pretty soon you will have made a significant improvement to the system. A new status quo will develop. Successful change has occurred, and people feel good about it, but things don't always work out that way.

Teachers are passionate people who don't like to be "shown up" by their peers. Sometimes when a teacher leader steps out in front, others don't follow and as a result that person gets too far ahead of the group. I have seen outstanding teachers in their zeal to lead and to have an impact on a school get too far out in front. The result? Their peers turned on them by not following, and this is the paradox with leadership— no matter how talented you are, you are not a leader if no one is following you. Skilled principals are able to keep entire staffs moving in a positive direction because they don't allow potential leaders to break from the pack.

CHANGE BRINGS CONFLICT

It is important for staff to get along and "fit in," but that doesn't happen without ongoing communication. The leadership literature talks about a concept called "straight talk," which is an organization's ability to allow issues to surface, own them, and resolve them so that they do not go underground and destroy the culture. Schools need a process by which people can share what they are really feeling and thinking without worrying if they offend someone.

An outstanding book on the market about teamwork is called *The Five Dysfunctions of a Team*, by Patrick Lencioni (2002). The book was not written for an education audience, but the principles apply wherever teams of people are trying to work together. One of the dysfunctions Lencioni discusses is an unwillingness to engage in conflict. Conflict is necessary for improvement and growth. Skilled leaders know how to manage conflict in positive ways. It is tricky business, but necessary. It has been my experience that educators, by our nature, tend to resist or avoid conflict whenever possible, and in the long run, burying issues is unhealthy for any organization.

> I was glad to read about the importance of conflict in a school in order to facilitate change. Most of us in our responses have indicated that we don't do well with conflict. Some of us, including myself, even avoid it at all costs. From the time we are little, conflict is something "bad." We should always get along with everyone, keep our mouths shut, and "be nice." One of the reasons that we as teachers did well in school is because we didn't rock the boat and did what we were told. I think it is possible to "be nice" and still be able to have conflict at school. Most of the great things at my school were brought about because an individual or group of people were not scared of conflict. (Middle School Teacher)

REFLECT AND RESPOND

What are some of the long-standing traditions in your school that no longer make sense? How are they hindering change and improvement? What can you do to help people begin to think differently about ineffective traditions?

TEACHER LEADER SCENARIO #8: CONTRACT NEGOTIATIONS

Contract negotiations in the school district are not going well. You feel caught in the crossfire between the district and union, and there is a lot of political activity going on. You would prefer just to close your door and teach, but the atmosphere in your building is making that difficult. People are taking sides. You can see the reasonableness of each side's concerns, and you don't want all of this to affect the students, but that is exactly what is happening. As a teacher leader in the school, what do you do? You are tired of being told if you take on that additional project without pay it will be "bad for teachers." What about the students? Who is sticking up for them?

Think about what you would do and then turn to appendix A: Teacher Leadership Scenario Responses for a suggestion about how to respond to the scenario listed above.

Appendix A

TEACHER LEADERSHIP
SCENARIO RESPONSES

Effective leadership in schools is complex. Most of the time there are no easy solutions. Decisions must be made quickly, and sometimes we will only find out how smart (or dumb) we are when the dust settles. The scenario suggestions on the following pages are certainly not the only way to approach the problems presented throughout this book. They are designed as a starting place for conversation. The whole is always greater than the sum of the parts. Wisdom is in the group; if you can get the group in the room to interact, the wisdom will be in the room, and you will be that much closer to better solutions.

STAFF ACTIVITY: TEACHER LEADERSHIP SCENARIOS

An effective way to use these suggestions with a staff is to copy each one on a separate piece of paper. At a staff meeting, have the teachers form into groups of four to six people. Pass out the teacher leadership scenarios. Have a teacher read a scenario to the group and ask the group to discuss some creative alternatives for addressing the problem. After they have had an opportunity to brainstorm, take volunteers to share proposed solutions. Once they have shared their ideas, read to the group the corresponding scenario response presented in this appendix. Make sure you create a safe environment before doing this activity, because staff members may recognize the behavior of their peers, which can be good if your environment is supportive but can go south in a hurry if people do not trust one another.

SCENARIO RESPONSE #1: AN UNINVOLVED STAFF

All teachers can and should lead, but whether we want to admit it or not, the behavior of a teaching staff is the direct result of the principal's leadership. If a principal is encouraging risk taking, committee involvement, innovation, shared leadership, and empowerment, then the staff will migrate toward those values. If you are the principal with an unmotivated staff, set an expectation for leadership by encouraging every teacher to be on at least one committee. Create committees if you have to so that there will be something appealing for everyone. But remember that leadership doesn't happen by putting people on committees—it happens when people get an opportunity to pursue their passions, so make the opportunities meaningful and authentic.

Get people involved. Value committee participation and publicly recognize teachers when they step into leadership roles. Every teacher has strengths. Encourage those strengths and use them as springboards for leadership opportunities. Over time your staff will be engaged and involved. If not, look in the mirror for ways you need to change and improve your leadership style and effectiveness. Read the book by Hess and Robinson, *Priority Leadership* (2006), which is a helpful handbook on leadership in schools from a systems perspective. If you are not sure what to do, ask for help. Never be too proud as a principal to ask for help.

The most effective principals realize they need coaching from others and actively seek out other skilled leaders from whom they can learn and grow. They do not try to make it on their own. Go to a conference. Read a book. I have seen disinterested, disengaged staffs suddenly become motivated and engaged—almost overnight—under new leadership or when old leaders find new fire. That doesn't mean you have to walk away from your staff to cause them to get more involved, but it does mean the transformation toward teacher leadership starts and ends with the principal.

STAFF ACTIVITY: WHAT'S IMPORTANT

Another effective way to engage a staff is find out what is important to them. Do the following activity: At a staff meeting on one side of the board write, "Decisions you make as teachers." Have them list all of the decisions they are responsible for and make on a regular basis. On the other side of the board write, "Decisions you would like to make." Start the list. This activity will be risky, but it will allow what your staff cares about to surface, and I am willing to bet that if you give them responsibility, ownership, and decision-making authority in some of these previous off-limits areas, you will see motivation immediately increase, and a whole new level of teacher leadership will emerge on your staff.

If you want to do more than push the envelope and think outside the box—if you want to rip the envelope and burn the box—then have your staff conduct the above activity with you outside of the room and come get you when they're done. You will be taking a bigger risk here, but you are guaranteed to get a pure glimpse of what your staff really values, and it is your best chance of getting the most wisdom from the group. Word of warning: Don't do this activity unless you are prepared to take action on at least a few of the items that get discussed.

SCENARIO RESPONSE #2:
INSPIRING INSTRUCTIONAL LEADERSHIP

If you are a teacher and find yourself in the midst of an unmotivated, bickering staff who seem to have no direction—or the wrong direction—don't let them get you down. The fabulous thing about teaching is that you can always close your door and teach, and sometimes the most effective thing you can do to motivate others is prove to them that it is possible to stay positive, motivated, and upbeat even when the school culture around you is negative.

When people go to work for Disney, they are taught to smile and treat every customer with kindness even if they have to grit their teeth to do it. In the world of teaching and learning, how much more important are our jobs? We work with children. Every student deserves to have a happy, motivated teacher, and do you know what? When people start acting like that, it tends to spread. Dee Hock (1999), founder of Visa, wrote that people should lead their supervisors. Your positive, can-do, upbeat attitude may be the one that makes the difference for your principal and helps him to improve. And if he gets better, the school culture can turn the corner.

Your other options are to wait it out for the next principal or look for a new school to work in. An unmotivated, disengaged, and negative staff can usually be traced to ineffective leadership. Principal turnover rate is high—especially in high schools. Odds are you will get a chance to work for someone else in the near future, and when that opportunity comes, be a part of the solution by participating on the interview team.

When you are on the interview team, remember that the number one indicator of someone's ability is not how he performs in the interview but how he performed in his previous jobs. Ask around. Go beyond reference lists and visit worksites if you can. Hiring a new principal is a lot more important than getting a new car. Don't be in a hurry. Shop around. This is your one opportunity to choose a family member. Do your research, and don't forget that sometimes the best candidates are right in your backyard, in your own school or district.

Even poor principals can look polished in an interview, and everyone has weaknesses. Those weaknesses are easy to spot in people you know. Don't be afraid to give the locals a chance if they have talent, relentless desire, and a willingness to learn. Perhaps all they need is some training and an opportunity.

If you decide that working in a new school is the way you want to go, open your eyes and be wise. Talk to teachers in the potential school where you want to work. Ask about leadership opportunities. Ask about principal and district office support, and whatever you decide to do, make a commitment to keep learning. Turn off the TV. Take a class. Design a new unit. Teach a new grade level. Get a master's degree. Go to a conference. Write something. Learning refreshes the brain. It makes you young. It restores you.

I know teachers who have never tired of learning new methods of teaching. They are constantly putting themselves out there to acquire new training and then applying that training in the classroom. When they approach me with another flyer in their hand, I know they have an idea, and smart principals support the people around them who are dedicated to learning.

Above all, be aware that the surest way of being in a school that fosters teacher leadership is to take what you know and become a principal yourself. School systems need quality leaders, and when you begin to understand the concept that effectively leading is merely a function of your willingness to learn and serve, the person in the mirror might just be the principal you are looking for.

SCENARIO RESPONSE #3: PRINCIPAL PETS

Jumping the leadership chain is rarely effective. You may get what you want in the short term, but the long-range payoff will be painful. What do you hope to gain by complaining to the superintendent about your principal and the lack of leadership opportunities at your school? Will your principal be likely to provide you opportunities after she gets in trouble, or is it more likely that a bigger wedge will develop in your relationship? If the principal is not making room for you on established committees, try to identify a need in the community or the school and propose a project you will lead to meet that need.

One teacher I know of who was looking for a way to lead simply got her class involved in picking up trash around the campus once a month. The trash was weighed, analyzed, written about, and discussed. The simple clean-up activity, which began as a way to serve, morphed into an integrated service-learning project that involved math, science, writing, speaking, and social studies standards.

If pursuing an informal role seems too daunting, look for other ways to exercise your leadership passion. There are usually opportunities to lead in most teaching associations. Whether it is being a building representative, committee member, or district team player, there are many ways to improve teaching conditions and student outcomes through professional association roles.

Most districts also have opportunities at the district level where the service of teachers is needed. Instead of engaging in a negative conversation about your principal with your superintendent, ask her about opportunities for service at the district level. What is your passion? What do you care deeply about? What is your vision for your classroom, the school, and the district? Communicate positively. Act passionately. Do something constructive. Eventually you will be recognized for your efforts, and more opportunities will come your way.

SCENARIO RESPONSE #4: TEAM CONFLICT

We have all been a part of ineffective teams that spend too much time complaining about problems rather than solving them, but people do not improve without training, and it is clear this team leader needs some training. The team needs training on two levels: improving the culture of the group and improving the skills of how they function as a team. It is wise for you not to step in with a solution. Building leadership capacity in teachers only comes as they learn how to work through difficulties, but they do need support. You can help by providing training on the expectations of grade-level teams. Expect two things from the team: positive relationships between the members and learning how to look at data systematically in order to make improvements. Provide training on those topics.

Begin the training by interviewing the team members separately and asking them questions about how the meetings are going, what is getting accomplished, how the group is functioning, and what team goals they have. Get suggestions from the team members on how to improve the group as well. It is important to focus the team on what they should be doing rather than what they shouldn't be doing. The backbiting and gossip will diminish when the group begins functioning as a data team. Teams are built through listening and supporting each other. When people work together effectively, they are able to build their confidence and support one another rather than become negative.

If you send them out for training, go with them or take staff from other high-functioning teams to attend a Professional Learning Community (PLC) conference together. When it comes to transformational change—and creating an effective team is transformational change—the worst thing you can do is name what you are doing. The moment you "begin" PLCs marks the beginning of the end. People resist change, and you have now named the enemy, and the danger is your

work may shift from continually improving the team process to starting the next new thing.

Make a commitment to improve and do not give up. Figure out a
way to measure the progress of the team's ability to develop positive relationships with each other and look at data systemically to make improvements. Teams of engineers at Toyota are trained to ask five "Why
Questions" for every problem they encounter. By doing so, they are able
to trace the root cause of complex problems, and usually those problems
exist between departments. As a result of their inquiry, they discover
deep solutions that lead to breakthrough improvements in quality.

Remember the old adage "You must inspect what you expect." As
you pay attention to developing high-performance learning teams, you
will see your teachers begin to reach their potential as leaders.

SCENARIO RESPONSE #5:
UNPRODUCTIVE STAFF MEETINGS

Schools are systems. Lesson one about systems: Leadership is responsible
for how they operate. If the system is functioning well, thank the leader.
If the system is dysfunctional, blame the leader. Teachers are parts in the
system. They are not responsible for staff meeting breakdowns. However, the whole concept behind teacher leadership is trying to discover
ways that teachers can step into leadership roles that will move them toward becoming architects of a functioning system rather than victims of
a dysfunctional one.

If staff doesn't look forward to staff meetings, the meetings are not
being run right. People hate meetings when they are unproductive and
irrelevant. People enjoy attending meetings when good things are happening and something gets done. If they don't want to be there, change
the content to make the meetings more relevant. Don't waste people's
time. Staff members who bring other work to meaningless meetings are
not being bad; they are being practical. They are trying to make full use
of the one resource that can't be carried over or saved—time. On the
other hand, staff members who bring newspapers to meetings are being
bad, and someone should talk to them.

It never bothers me when teachers bring schoolwork to meetings. I always see that behavior as a sign of intelligence and productivity, and the message is loud and clear to me: "Be relevant with my time. If you are not relevant, I will create my own relevancy." I enjoy the challenge. No matter what, I want people leaving my meetings thinking the time was well spent, and if that means I provided a little time for them to get some work done, so be it.

The chief purpose of meetings is to discover the collective wisdom in the room so that better decisions can be made (Reeves, 2006). Structure your staff meetings to be productive or stop having them. Incorporate training into staff meetings so that people begin to realize you value training and learning above whining and griping. Wise leaders write down their ideas and bring proposals to meetings that staff can respond to so forward movement is continually generated. They also create a time and space to air grievances and work through conflict, but they do not allow whining or negative fantasies to dominate staff meetings.

SCENARIO RESPONSE #6: LEAVING THE PACK

The first thing you should do is talk to your principal and let her know the rumor you heard and ask for some advice. Most rumors are the result of poor communication, so there is a strong possibility that the information you are getting via the grapevine is not very accurate. It is never a good idea to base professional decisions on rumors or grapevine knowledge. When teachers pursue leadership roles, it is good for kids. It is the right thing to do, and it is much better to base your decisions on what is right than on other people's perceptions of your behavior. If you have the time and passion for it, you should absolutely take the opportunity to lead a district seminar—and not feel bad about it.

If it is true that there are bad feelings from staff members about your leadership roles, the best thing to do is talk to those people individually. Increased communication and acts of service will overcome negative feelings. As long as your schedule can take it, keep stepping into leadership roles. It is the right thing to do.

From the principal's perspective, the danger of one or only a few teachers stepping forward into leadership roles is that those people may over time burn out or distance themselves too far from the rest of the staff, and then there will be problems. If the majority of staff members are not leading in some way, the few that are will begin wearing targets on their backs, which is never a good thing.

Feelings of favoritism, competition, and jealously will emerge, and the school culture will begin to erode. It is the principal's job to ensure that leadership is spread throughout the school so that the entire group moves forward together at a faster pace. In this way, the group never loses sight of the pacesetters, and in an ideal school, the role of pacesetting is constantly rotating so that no one gets burned out.

SCENARIO RESPONSE #7: NEW KID ON THE BLOCK

Starting a new job is never easy, and there is always a season of adjustment as you get used to the new setting. If you are a first- or second-year teacher, chances are you have so much to learn and figure out in your own classroom that worrying about how people may perceive you is not time well spent. Many districts have some type of mentoring options available for new teachers, and usually those programs are as effective as the energy you put into them. Get involved and take full advantage of the opportunities. Make connections and find support any way you can.

Even the grumpiest of people like to talk about themselves and have someone listen to them. Since you are new to the building, you will be able to learn a lot from those who have been there for a while. Spend more time listening than talking—especially if you know they aren't very receptive to your ideas. Most seasoned teachers have seen so many bright people and shiny ideas come and go they are naturally resistant and skeptical to anything that is new or different, and a bridge of trust and communication must be built first and foremost before your ideas will reach them.

Remember, too, that the most effective leadership is built on a foundation of service. Serve your colleagues any and every way you can. Commit yourself to teaching and learning. Take a class. Implement your ideas in your classroom first and obtain results. Get involved in as many district-level trainings and activities as possible. Chances are good the other new teachers in the building are having similar feelings. Get together and support one another. Over the course of time, you will be the seasoned teacher. When that time arrives, remember how you were treated and make a decision to be supportive and inclusive when fresh people arrive with their crazy new ideas.

If you are a principal, remember your new teachers. New teachers need constant support and encouragement to be successful. Studies indicate that nearly half of them will leave the teaching profession within their first five years, and many of them will leave because the school system is not responsive to change and innovation (Palmer, 2007). If your district doesn't have a formal way of supporting them, devise an informal way yourself. Every time a new person enters your system, he or she brings new ideas and is able to see things you cannot. Take time to listen, because in a year or two they will be acclimated to your system, and their passion for new ideas and willingness to share them will fade.

SCENARIO RESPONSE #8: CONTRACT NEGOTIATIONS

Labor negotiations can be absolute culture killers. This book has emphasized again and again the connection between culture and teacher leadership. When administration and teachers are putting a lot of energy into negative labor negotiations, there is little time for anything else. Whatever the potential savings of a strike is paid for by the culture of the district and school, and once culture takes a hit, only time and trust will build it back up again. Even threats of striking can leave scars that will take time to heal.

At the same time, it is important to realize that the balance of power unions create in public schools is healthy. I have spent time with teachers who taught in schools prior to unions or are currently working in private or charter schools where unions do not exist. Many of them are underpaid and undertrained. Having worked in both private and public schools, it is my experience that the level of teaching commitment in public schools exceeds what is required from those working in private schools. State and federal accountability, additional licensure requirements, and the opportunity to earn a living wage as a result of union bargaining have a lot to do it.

In times of high stress, it is important to find a few like-minded colleagues. Get together and talk through your feelings and what you are thinking. There is no easy answer to political dilemmas—especially when children become pawns for both sides. In the meantime, pour your energy into your classroom. In the worst of times, when the school culture is eroding, your students deserve the best you have to offer. Directing positive energy toward your students and commiserating with like-minded friends and family will help you know what to do in the midst of the conflict. Whatever you decide to do, make sure you act with integrity even if those around you are not. Regardless of the cost or outcome, you will never regret keeping your integrity intact.

Appendix B

TEACHER LEADER
INTERNET RESOURCES

Throughout my teaching and research and on the subject of teacher leadership, I have greatly benefited from a variety of websites. These websites and their descriptors are written here to encourage you to see what is already happening around the world concerning the topic of teacher leadership. Students in my online courses through Oregon State University discovered many of these sites.

www.breakthroughschools.org

The Breakthrough Schools website contains sections on school culture, teacher leadership, and a bulletin board where teachers can share successes with others in the field.

www.learningfirst.org/publications/districts/

The Learning First Alliance is dedicated to strengthening the public school experience for every child. This webpage highlights districtwide reform by describing what districts can do to improve instruction and achievement in all schools.

www.schoolculture.net

An outstanding website built on the philosophy that school culture is critical to student achievement and high levels of teacher leadership.

www.bigpicture.org/

A reform movement that puts students and teachers in the center through a philosophy of creating small schools that promote personalized education programs unique for each student. There are dozen of Big Picture schools throughout the country.

www.freedomwritersfoundation.org/

Freedom Writers was founded by Erin Gruwell, a teacher who transformed a hopeless urban classroom into a beacon of achievement and learning. Her story was made into a motion picture and is an example of teacher leadership. It demonstrates what is possible when one person is willing to do whatever it takes to make positive, meaningful connections with her students and develop curriculum that is based on student needs.

www.annenberginstitute.org

The Annenberg Institute is a leader of the Critical Friends movement. This website provides resources to support the developing of professional learning communities and especially items related to the CFG movement.

www.hobartshakespeareans.org

One of the most remarkable stories in our generation is that of teacher Rafe Esquith, who began teaching in 1981 in Los Angeles at Hobart Elementary School where all of his students are on free and reduced lunch. In this public school classroom, students voluntarily start class at 6:30 A.M. and stay until 5 P.M. Every year the class produces an unabridged Shakespearean play. The author of two books, Esquith is truly an inspiration, yet very down-to-earth. His story proves that even in the most trying of situations, all students can learn and achieve at high levels. He continues to teach at Hobart.

http://cse.edc.org/products/teacherleadership/mentoring.asp

Resources for Teacher Leadership is an extraordinary website. The site was developed with the help of the Presidential Awards for Excellence in Mathematics and Science Teaching. The site is organized into six leadership areas—making presentations, writing for publication, reaching out to the community, mentoring and coaching, providing professional development, and supporting preservice educators.

www.ctl.vcu.edu

Another organization that promotes teacher leadership is the Center for Teacher Leadership (CTL). The goal of this organization is to provide training, resources, and support for teacher leaders. It also serves as a mediator for teachers and policymakers throughout the state of Virginia.

www.ed.gov/pubs/TeachersLead/index.html

The National Teacher Forum was created in 1998. It contains great information that aspiring teacher leaders need to know. It provides short and easy-to-understand answers to some basic questions. This site gives the reader a good idea why teacher leadership is important.

www.edst.educ.ubc.ca/courses/EADM532/Barth.pdf

Roland Barth's article "The Teacher Leader" is currently out of print, but it can be obtained at this site.

www.educationworld.com

Education World is full of teacher resources including a large variety of searchable lesson plans that are tied to standards.

www.ericdigests.org/pre-9219/skills.htm

This resource is an article about how to develop teacher leaders. It is important because it discusses what needs to be in place in order for teacher leadership to occur in a school. It also addresses what teacher leaders need in order to be successful.

www.makingstandardswork.com

Author and reformer Douglas Reeves manages this website. He is a strong proponent of shared leadership and author of several books dedicated to school improvement, including *The Learning Leader* (2006) and *Accountability for Learning* (2004).

www.mentors.net/03library/boston.html

Continuous improvement in teaching and learning is the expectation for every school and teacher in the Boston district. What teachers know and can do is essential in accelerating the academic achievement of students. The overarching purpose of the Mentor Program is to rapidly develop the professional skills, knowledge, and expertise of beginning teachers for improved teaching and learning.

www.nsdc.org/library/leaders/teachers.cfm

This is a great link to various articles dealing with the effectiveness and importance of teacher leadership.

www.nsrfharmony.org

National School Reform Faculty site provides many resources and training for the Critical Friends Movement.

www.ous.edu/aca/SAELP/OEA_ldrshp.pdf

This 14-page summary by Sam Miller for the Oregon Education Association is useful as an overview of teacher leadership. It is a great site for teachers who are involved in mentoring activities.

www.stpt.usf.edu/emailheaders/coeleadership.htm

This site is through the University of South Florida and is dedicated to promoting a workshop called the Teacher Leadership Institute, being led by Ann Lieberman. The Teacher Leadership Institute is a two-day seminar in which teachers and administrators participate in interactive sessions to explore the role of teachers as leaders. The teacher–administrator teams use teacher leadership research on best practices to develop plans to foster schoolwide teacher leadership.

www.teacherleaders.org

The Teacher Leaders Network (TLN) was created to help facilitate teachers that are trying to initiate change within their schools. With the help of modern technological advancements, teachers from different parts of the United States can connect and discuss plans for change. The TLN is connected to the Center for Teacher Quality organization.

www.teacherquality.org

The Center for Teacher Quality is the founding organization of the Teacher Leaders Network. The Center for Teacher Quality is an organization that was founded in the mid-1990s to serve as a front-runner in educational research and policy reforms and as a center to improve the standards of the education system at every level.

www.yale.edu/ynhti/pubs/A22/Cooke.html

This article addresses some of the questions administrators might ask: Why Do We Lose Teacher-Leaders? Why Have We Retained the Ones Who Have Stayed? and How Do We Find New Ones? You will appreciate the real-life examples used to illustrate teacher leadership from an administrative perspective.

www.ncsl.org.uk/media/1D5/A9/teacher-leadership-summary.pdf

This article is well documented with the authors' research and gives insight into what teacher leadership means and what others in the education field have discovered. The article provides an interesting definition of teacher leadership, what it requires, and how to foster it in schools.

www.newteacher.com/index.html

The First Days of School Foundation, which was created by Harry and Rosemary Wong, includes many articles and helpful strategies for teachers beginning their careers.

www.ascd.org/portal/site/ascd/menuitem.a4dbd0f2c4f9b94cdeb3ffdb6 2108a0c/

This newsletter is just one of the resources available from the ASCD, Association for Supervision and Curriculum Development, which is an international nonprofit organization with members from over 135 countries. They offer information to teachers, administrators, and any other types of educators about topics such as professional development and leadership development. Their homepage is located at www.ascd.org.

www.pdkintl.org/kappan/k0106gui.htm

This site provides information about instructional coaching. It describes the differences between change coaches and content coaches. It also points out research that shows a positive link between coaching and increased student achievement.

www.iel.org/

The Institute for Educational Leadership sponsors this site, and the organization recognizes the challenges involved with teacher leadership and offers suggestions to adjust to new challenges that emerge.

www.cepa.gse.rutgers.edu/whatweknow.pdf

This article documents the benefits of teacher leadership in schools and shows that teacher leadership has significant effects on student learning.

www.education-world.com/a_issues/chat/chat076.shtml

Education World offers a huge amount of articles, many of which relate to teacher leadership. One article especially interesting is titled "National Teacher Calls for More Teacher Leaders," by Dr. Betsy Rogers, the National 2003 Teacher of the Year. Near the end of the article, Dr. Rogers talks about the message she wishes she could send out to teachers, "All children can learn. All teachers can lead."

www.ed.gov/pubs/TeachersLead/forms.html

This site lists 14 ways teachers can lead. If you're looking for a leadership role to step into at school, but aren't sure exactly how to do it, or where to start, this website offers up some suggestions. Each suggestion is paired with a real-life situation where a teacher stepped into this leadership role and made something happen.

www.middleweb.com/mentoring.html

A website that offers a wide variety of articles and links to foster the creation of successful mentoring programs. Articles and links are found from various other sources including The Teachers Network, Edutopia, ASCD, Classroom Leadership Online, etc. This website is a great place to start if you are looking for a mentor teacher, thinking about being a mentor teacher, and/or wondering if the mentor relationship you currently have is the most effective model.

http://www.k-12.state.tn.us/tpd/teacher.htm

This website is helpful and informative and is the official website of Tennessee. It addresses Teacher Leadership Development and the background behind their staff development program.

http://www.iel.org/pubs/schoolleaders.pdf

This website has an article entitled "Preparing and Supporting School Leaders: The Importance of Assessment and Evaluation."

www.iel.org/programs/21st/reports/teachlearn.pdf

"Redefining the Teacher as Leader" is the result of a panel of 13 teachers, administrators, and professors discussing the role of leadership in teaching. It was sponsored by the Institute of Educational Leadership, a nonprofit organization that has been around for 35 years. This 36-page report covers roadblocks to leadership, teacher training that strengthens leadership roles like National Board Certification, and questions to use to encourage discussions about leadership.

www.stenhouse.com/pdfs/0343ch08/pdf

"Teacher Leadership: Switching Roles" is chapter 8 of Diane Sweeney's book, *Learning along the Way: Professional Development by and for Teachers*. In this chapter, Sweeney acknowledges that the skills required to lead and teach adults are different than the skills we use to teach children.

www.csupomona.edu/~ijtl/

The International Journal of Teacher Leadership was launched to promote teacher leadership around the world. It is a scholarly online journal that publishes articles related to teacher leadership.

www.cstp-wa.org/Navigational/Teacherleadership

The Center for Strengthening the Teaching Profession website offers articles that focus on research, case studies, and other forums for teacher leaders to share their findings. The site promotes a series of workshops for teachers in leadership positions.

www.edutopia.org/php/article.php?id=Art_166

The George Lucas Educational Foundation was founded in 1991. It is a nonprofit organization that encourages any innovative programs created in schools. This website is very easy to navigate and has all the bells and whistles that keep you coming back for more.

www.chalkboardproject.org/index.php

Launched in March 2004, the Chalkboard Project exists to inspire Oregonians to do what it takes to make their K–12 public schools among the nation's best. Chalkboard aims to help create a more informed and engaged public who understands and addresses the tough choices and trade-offs required to build strong schools.

www.centerforcsri.org/

The Center for CSRI is funded through the U.S. Department of Education, and their site contains links to many other great resources, as well as their own publications on school improvement topics and strategies for school reform. The site contains a library of many research-based articles on the topic of school improvement.

www.nsba.org/sbot/toolkit/index.html

Educational Leadership Toolkit (National School Board Association) is a rich resource. You will find an entire section devoted to teacher leadership that has some truly innovative ideas including a chance to answer questions to determine your own abilities as a leader.

www.2.bc.edu/~hargrean/docs/seven_principles.pdf

"Seven Principles of Sustainable Leadership" by Andy Hargreaves and Dean Fink is an interesting article that discusses the outcome of a study on how leadership can be sustained over time.

www.nwrel.org

Northwest Regional Education Laboratory is an excellent resource that focuses on the Northwest region of the country. The laboratory provides products, news, and workshops along with resources focusing on improving classroom teaching and learning; improving schools and districts; communication among schools, family, and community; and research evaluation and assessment. There is a lot of information that is usable and relevant.

www.nlns.org/NLWeb/Criteria.jsp

A list of criteria used to assess candidates for the program New Leaders for New Schools. This list is quite comprehensive when asking,

What are the traits of a leader? New Leaders for New Schools is an attempt to take teacher leaders, train them, and have each individual open a school using a new philosophy with both students and faculty.

www.envisionprojects.org/

Envision Schools is a nonprofit-based charter school group. Many of these schools employ project-based learning that in turn involves the students more completely in the learning experience. Teachers must share, integrate, and lead in order to have this type of learning be successful.

www.sedl.org/change/issues/issues44.html

This article will take you step-by-step through what teacher leadership is and why it is important. It also discussion what teacher leaders do and the benefits of pursuing leadership.

http://www.teacherscount.org/teacher/topic/topic-rogers.shtml

The article is written in question-answer format. It not only explains what teacher leadership is, but addresses the kinds of programs that can be implemented to prepare teachers for leadership roles.

REFERENCES

American Association of School Administrators (AASA) Communications. (2007). *No Child Law Faces Medley of Changes.* Retrieved March 29, 2007, from www.stateline.org.

Appleby, J. (1998). *Becoming Critical Friends: Reflections of an NSRF Coach.* Providence, RI: Annenberg Institute for School Reform at Brown University.

Autry, J. A. (2001). *The Servant Leader: How to Build a Creative Team, Develop Great Morale, and Improve Bottom-Line Performance.* New York: Three Rivers Press.

Bambino, D. (2002, March). Redesigning Professional Development: Critical Friends. *Educational Leadership, 59*(6): 25–27.

Barr, R. D., & Parrett, W. D. (2003). *Saving Our Students, Saving Our Schools: 50 Proven Strategies for Revitalizing At-Risk Students and Low-Performing Schools.* Thousand Oaks, CA: Corwin Press.

Barth, R. (1999). *The Teacher Leader.* Providence: Rhode Island Foundation.

———. (2001). *Learning by Heart.* San Francisco: Jossey-Bass.

Blanchard, K. (2003). *Servant Leader.* Nashville: Thomas Nelson.

Bonstingl, J. J. (2001). *Schools of Quality* (3rd ed.). Thousand Oaks, CA: Corwin Press.

Cushman, K. M. (1998). *How Friends Can Be Critical as Schools Make Essential Changes.* Oxon Hill, MD: Coalition of Essential Schools.

Danielson, C. (2006). *Teacher Leadership that Strengthens Professional Practice.* Alexandria, VA: Association for Supervision and Curriculum Development.

Deming, W. E. (1986). *Out of the Crisis.* Cambridge: Massachusetts Institute of Technology Press.

Dufour, R., & Eaker, R. (1998). *Professional Learning Communities at Work: Best Practices for Enhancing Student Achievement.* Bloomington, IN: National Educational Service.

Golly, A., & Sprague, J. (2005). *Best Behavior: Building Positive Behavior Support in Schools.* Longmont, CO: Sopris West.

Graves, B., & Wood, S. O. (2006, September 25). If They Finish in High School, They Stumble in College. *The [Portland] Oregonian.*

Greenleaf, R. (1977). *Servant Leadership: A Journey into the Nature of Legitimate Power and Greatness.* Mahwah, NJ: Paulist Press.

Hasbrouck, J., & Denton, C. (2005). *The Reading Coach: A How-To Manual for Success.* Longmont, CO: Sopris West.

Hess, R. T. (2005). *Excellence, Equity, Efficiency: How Principals and Policymakers Can Survive the Triangle of Tension.* Lanham, MD: Rowman & Littlefield Education.

Hess, R. T., & Robinson, J. W. (2006). *Priority Leadership: Generating School and District Improvement through Systemic Change.* Lanham, MD: Rowman & Littlefield Education.

Hock, D. (1999). *Birth of the Charodic Age.* San Francisco: Jossey-Bass.

Hunter, J. C. (1998). *The Servant: A Simple Story about the True Essence of Leadership.* New York: Crown Business.

Jones, J. H. (Ed.). (1994). *Prisoners of Time: School and Programs Making Time Work for Students and Teachers.* Darby, PA: Diane Publishing.

Lencioni, P. M. (2002). *The Five Dysfunctions of a Team: A Leadership Fable.* San Francisco: Jossey-Bass.

McEwan, E. (2002). *The Ten Traits of Highly Effective Teachers: How to Hire, Coach, and Mentor Successful Teachers.* Thousand Oaks, CA: Corwin Press.

Merideth, E. M. (2007). *Leadership Strategies for Teachers* (2nd ed.). Thousand Oaks, CA: Corwin Press.

Metlife. (2003). *The MetLife Survey of the American Teacher, 2003: An Examination of School Leadership.* Long Island City, NY: Author.

Moss-Kanter, R. (2004). *Confidence: How Winning Streaks and Losing Streaks Begin and End.* New York: Crown.

National Council on Economic Education (NCEE). (2007). Effectiveness of Reading and Mathematics Software Products: Findings from the First Student Cohort. *National Council on Economic Education.* Retrieved April 4, 2007, from http://ies.gov/ncee/pubs/20074005/.

National School Reform Faculty (NSRF). (2007). Critical Friends Research. *National School Reform Faculty.* Retrieved April 7, 2007, from www.nsfrharmony.org/faq.html#1.

Palmer, K. (2007). Why Teachers Quit. *Teacher Magazine.* Retrieved June 15, 2007, from www.teachermagazine.org/tm/articles/2007/05/01/06quit.h.18.html.

Reeves, D. (2006). *The Learning Leader: How to Focus School Improvement for Better Results.* Alexandria, VA: Association for Supervision and Curriculum Development.

Robbins, P. (2005). *The Leader's Role in Building Professional Learning Communities.* Presented at Leading and Learning—Focusing on Improvement. February 2, 2007.

Rothstein, R., & Jacobsen, R. (2007, March). A Test of Time: Unchanged Priorities for Student Outcomes. *The School Administrator, 64*(3): 35–39.

Schoenbach, R., Greenleaf, C., Cziko, C., & Hurwitz, L. (2000). *Reading for Understanding.* San Francisco: Jossey-Bass.

Senge, P. (1994). *The Fifth Discipline.* New York: Doubleday.

ABOUT THE AUTHOR

Robert Hess lives with his wife, Jeanne, and four children (Daniel, Jacob, Grace, and Truman) on a five-acre farm in Lebanon, Oregon. *Follow the Teacher* is Rob's third book. He has worked in schools for over 20 years and has taught in both inner-city urban schools and rural schools at the middle and high school levels. As an administrator, he has worked at the high school, middle school, and K–8 levels.

Rob is currently the Student Achievement Leader for Springfield Public Schools in Springfield, Oregon. Springfield is the 11th-largest school district in Oregon, and Rob is responsible for helping the district's 25 schools develop and implement school improvement visions that will have a direct impact on student achievement.

He completed a doctorate of education degree at the University of Oregon in 2003 and has taught graduate-level education courses at the University of Oregon, Oregon State University, and Lewis and Clark College. During his career as an administrator, he has conducted several workshops and presentations at state and national conferences.

He has developed a website (www.breakthroughschools.org) to support school improvement and encourage networking among educators. In 2005 his first book was published by Scarecrow Education, *Excellence, Equity, Efficiency: How Principals Can Survive the Triangle of Tension*, and in 2006 he coauthored *Priority Leadership* with Dr. James Robinson.

Rob's expertise is school improvement through high-quality teaching and learning, leadership, systemic change, student achievement, mediation, meeting facilitation, and quality through continuous progress. He conducts workshops and professional development on these topics and can be reached at robhess1@mac.com.

LaVergne, TN USA
13 January 2010
169961LV00002B/22/P

9 781578 866762